Sponsorship

This is a book about generosity. It is a book about the life and legacy of local philanthropist Alice Keck Park who, upon her death in 1977, left the largest charitable bequest in Santa Barbara history: $20 million dollar bequest to Cottage Hospital, the Santa Barbara Museum of Art, and the Santa Barbara Botanic Garden.

She also left a very special gift to the entire community—a full block of prime downtown real estate to be developed and maintained as a public garden. Named in her honor, Alice Keck Park Memorial Garden is the crown jewel in the City of Santa Barbara's exceptional park system. Due to the generosity of one public spirited woman, the people of Santa Barbara are able to enjoy an exceptional urban landscape in perpetuity.

The Santa Barbara Botanic Garden is honoring this extraordinary generosity with the publication of this book. *Alice's Garden* celebrates the life of Alice Keck Park and the memorial garden bearing her name. This beautiful book by Anne-Marie Castleberg is a tribute to this woman and to the philanthropic spirit that so exemplifies our entire community. It is this generosity of spirit that has made this book possible.

With deep appreciation, the Botanic Garden wishes to acknowledge the **Helen Clay Frick Foundation of Pittsburgh, PA; the Park and Recreation Community Foundation and the Santa Barbara Parks and Recreation Department; Santa Barbara Beautiful; Santa Barbara Bank & Trust; and Mid-State Bank** for their generous support of this publishing effort.

To those who contributed to this publication, and to all who support philanthropic works in Santa Barbara, thank you.

Sponsorship

This is a book about generosity. It is a book about the life and legacy of local philanthropist Alice Keck Park who, upon her death in 1977, left the largest charitable bequest in Santa Barbara history: $20 million dollar bequest to Cottage Hospital, the Santa Barbara Museum of Art, and the Santa Barbara Botanic Garden.

She also left a very special gift to the entire community—a full block of prime downtown real estate to be developed and maintained as a public garden. Named in her honor, Alice Keck Park Memorial Garden is the crown jewel in the City of Santa Barbara's exceptional park system. Due to the generosity of one public spirited woman, the people of Santa Barbara are able to enjoy an exceptional urban landscape in perpetuity.

The Santa Barbara Botanic Garden is honoring this extraordinary generosity with the publication of this book. Alice's Garden celebrates the life of Alice Keck Park and the memorial garden bearing her name. This beautiful book by Anne-Marie Castleberg is a tribute to this woman and to the philanthropic spirit that so exemplifies our entire community. It is this generosity of spirit that has made this book possible.

With deep appreciation, the Botanic Garden wishes to acknowledge the Helen Clay Frick Foundation of Pittsburgh, PA; the Park and Recreation Community Foundation and the Santa Barbara Parks and Recreation Department; Santa Barbara Beautiful; Santa Barbara Bank & Trust; and Mid-State Bank for their generous support of this publishing effort.

To those who contributed to this publication, and to all who support philanthropic works in Santa Barbara, thank you.

alice's garden

for Grant

Published by

The Santa Barbara Botanic Garden

1212 Mission Canyon Road
Santa Barbara, California 93105

To order additional copies of the book, call 805-682-4726 ext. 112
or visit us on-line at www.sbbg.org

Alice's Garden
Alice Keck Park Memorial Garden, Santa Barbara, California
by Anne-Marie Castleberg
Photography by Ralph A. Clevenger

www.alicesgarden.info

First Edition

ISBN 0-916436-05-5
Library of Congress Control Number: 2005931715

Design, Digital Production and Printing by Media 27, Inc., Santa Barbara, California

WWW.MEDIA27.COM

Printed and bound in the United States

Alice Keck Park Memorial Garden, Santa Barbara, California

alice's garden

Anne-Marie Castleberg
Photography by Ralph A. Clevenger

*D*edicated to the memory of Alice Keck Park, whose generous gifts to Santa Barbara have left an indelible mark on the entire community. She gave us not only this garden, but also richly endowed four organizations in the city: Cottage Hospital, the Santa Barbara Art Museum, the Santa Barbara Botanic Garden, and the Santa Barbara Humane Society.

This book is also dedicated to Reginald Faletti and Elizabeth de Forest, who both had the vision to help create this horticultural landmark.

Erythrina coralloides (African Coral Tree)

contents

foreword

In 1975, the Board of Trustees of the Santa Barbara Botanic Garden entered an important agreement with the City of Santa Barbara whereby the Botanic Garden would assume the responsibility, as per the wishes of Alice Keck Park, for the development of the landscape design and construction of a newly proposed park to be located on the site of the old El Mirarsol Hotel which Mrs. Park had anonymously purchased and donated for that purpose. The Botanic Garden would also be the new park's continuing landscape consultant.

The Botanic Garden was honored to be chosen by Mrs. Park and to serve her memory, and the community, in this capacity. Her generous financial support of the Botanic Garden has significantly contributed to our ability to further our mission. We were pleased to be given the opportunity to further this important goal of hers, to offer all our citizens a garden to use in perpetuity.

Also, we owe our own beginning eighty years ago to the generosity of another woman with the foresight to preserve open space for public enjoyment, aesthetics, recreation, and education, Anna Dorinda Blaksley Bliss. We found poignancy in this striking similarity.

We embraced our role in the development of this new park—soon to be named Alice Keck Park Memorial Garden—with enthusiasm, bringing to it experience, knowledge, diligence, and professional expertise.

Since that time, the Botanic Garden has worked closely with the City of Santa Barbara to develop and maintain a beautiful garden that is true to its donor's wishes and to the needs of the Santa Barbara community. The Board of Trustees' choice of landscape designer Grant Castleberg was wise and warranted. Castleberg's brilliant design combines botanical and horticultural knowledge to create an exquisite urban retreat that edifies both the mind and the spirit. A public park, Alice Keck Park Memorial Garden is informal yet intimate and offers visitors a serene environment in which to stroll or picnic, enjoy quiet contemplation, learn about plant life, or simply experience beauty. The Botanic Garden continues to advise and oversee this dynamic garden's design and maintenance in conjunction with the City of Santa Barbara's Parks and Recreation Department.

Our commitment and caring stewardship extends to the publication of this exciting and beautiful new book, *Alice's Garden.*

When Anne-Marie Castleberg approached the Santa Barbara Botanic Garden to discuss the book she was writing about Alice Keck Park and the beautiful Memorial Garden that bears her name, our interest immediately piqued. A book on this garden's history and that of its benefactress seemed not only an excellent idea, but one long overdue. This exquisite garden, the jewel in the crown of the City of Santa Barbara's excellent park system, is much loved by our citizens, yet few know its history or that of the woman whose generosity made it all possible.

As the thirtieth anniversary of the Botanic Garden's role as landscape steward for the Memorial Garden approached, the time for such a book seemed particularly apt. A writer and the wife of the Memorial Garden's landscape architect, Anne-Marie Castleberg was particularly qualified to undertake this important project.

The result is magnificent. Mrs. Castleberg's well-researched biography of Alice Keck Park fills in many of the missing facts of this reclusive woman's life, rendering a more complete picture of an interesting and complex human being. Her thorough history of the landscape design from inception through construction and completion offers insights into the designer's artistic and intellectual concepts as well as descriptions of plant displays. The poetry and prose selections woven through the narrative capture the essence of the garden's spirit. Coupled with the stunning photographs by Ralph A. Clevenger, her writing vividly illustrates a garden brought to life.

The Santa Barbara Botanic Garden is proud to be the publisher of this important addition to Santa Barbara history. The book is a milestone marking our commitment to Alice Keck Park, her beautiful Memorial Garden, the citizens of our community, and our partnership with the City of Santa Barbara. Begun thirty years ago, this partnership and the expert stewardship it provides will continue, guarantying the future of this garden paradise for generations to come.

Gary Gallup, Chair
Santa Barbara Botanic Garden
Board of Trustees
2005

Anne Jones, Board Member
Santa Barbara Botanic Garden
Board of Trustees
1975

introduction

Astelia chathamica (Silver Spear), *Cassia leptophylla* (Gold Medallion Tree), *Miscanthus sinensis* (Maiden Grass)

There was a time when man lived close to nature. For most of the modern world, that time is long gone. Yet in the heart of Santa Barbara, a celebrated horticultural park delights casual visitors and dedicated gardeners alike. Beneath stately palms a diverse array of shrubs, bulbs, and groundcovers blankets the soil. In every season brilliant color abounds. Each spring orange clivias blaze beneath an ancient tea tree. During summer a yellow-blossomed cassia puts on a stunning show. The foliage of Chinese pistache trees adds to the vivid hues of fall, and in winter the spindly silvery-white trunks of the *Toona sinensis* elicit curiosity. The scene in Alice Keck Park Memorial Garden is constantly changing, and each return visit offers a new experience.

Stand Still. The trees ahead and bushes beside you
Are not lost. Wherever you are is called Here,
And you must treat it as a powerful stranger,
Must ask permission to know it and be known.
The forest breathes. Listen. It answers,
I have made this place around you,
If you leave it you may come back again, saying Here.
No two trees are the same to Raven.
No two branches are the same to Wren.
If what a tree or bush does is lost on you,
You are surely lost. Stand still. The forest knows
Where you are. You must let it find you.

DAVID WAGONER

Aerial view of Alice Keck Park Memorial Garden.

has been dubbed the "Jewel of the Pacific" and the "American Riviera." Alice Keck Park died shortly before "her" garden (as she referred to it in her last conversation with her sister) was completed, and when trustees for the park learned of her bequests to Santa Barbara's Cottage Hospital, Museum of Art, Botanic Garden, and Humane Society, they decided to name the horticultural sanctuary in her honor. Now, affectionately nicknamed "Alice," this park is a "gem within a gem," a precious heirloom. It remains the most visible symbol of Alice Keck Park's generosity to her city, though in monetary value it is the least significant of her contributions.

Her gift was intended for ordinary people, a place for a nature-break for the soul, a brown bag picnic lunch, or a few moments of solitude. Three decades after the park was presented to the city, its popularity continues to grow. This enchanting garden has no playgrounds, no athletic fields, and none of the busyness of most city parks, yet year after year it is voted Santa Barbara's favorite. Through the vision of the landscape architect, the once flat, four-acre block has been transformed into separate "rooms," discrete spaces separated from each other by greenery and foliage. These churchlike niches with sunlight streaming through canopies of leaves are conducive to silence and serenity, reminiscent of convent gardens and the traditional cloisters of the Middle Ages.

Decomposed granite paths, like hard-packed sand, meander through groves of mature trees and among dense shrubbery, connecting the garden's rooms. Ocher-toned rocks around the pond and along the banks of a stream reflect the sandstone of the mountains beyond. A wide swath of hot-pink bougainvillea borders the southern boundary, dramatically separating the visitor from traffic on the street.

*L*ittle is known about the generous heiress who, twenty-five years ago, donated this refuge, yet who wished to remain anonymous. Undoubtedly, Alice Keck Park found solace and peace in quiet places, away from the crowd. She loved natural beauty— the wild meadow at the Santa Barbara Botanic Garden, the alpine landscapes of Northern Italy, and the mountains of Colorado. She understood the healing power of nature and decided to share the thing that gave her the most joy. During her lifetime she chose to give a park—not build a museum or a fancy home for herself.

When she died in 1977, Alice Keck Park bequeathed her entire estate —more than fifty million dollars—to four charities in the city that

In the bucolic pond, enormous koi glide silently among the flat round leaves of pale, pastel water lilies; families of ducks slide across the glassy surface; and turtles take the sun on tawny boulders. A ramped spiral path leads to a shady haven atop a mound, with a sundial, that rises above the far side of the water. There, a low wall forms a circular area ideal for a moment of reflection.

On almost any weekend of the year, there's a wedding in the park, tai-chi on the lawn, and families picnicking. Always there is bird-song, sometimes music. An early morning jogger pauses to witness the sun's first rays transform the scene: jagged mountain peaks emerge from the darkness, and the tips of trees catch the light. In the late afternoon, as birds head home across the fading sky, shadows lengthen, trees and mountains fade, till finally night erases the brilliance and color of the day.

On the sandstone wall encircling the sundial, a bronze plaque lists the names of the people most responsible for Alice Keck Park Memorial Garden: Besides Alice Keck Park, there are Elizabeth de Forest, Grant Castleberg, Reginald Faletti, and Francis Price. Elizabeth de Forest was the widow of noted Santa Barbara landscape architect Lockwood de Forest and an ardent horticulturist herself. One of the few people who actually knew the reclusive heiress, she was entrusted to act as her representative. Elizabeth's vision for the space became a pivotal factor in establishing the guidelines for the park as we know it. As a member of the Santa Barbara Botanic Garden board of trustees, she selected Grant Castleberg, my husband, to design the project. Though a relatively young landscape architect, he had already won a number of awards, and his design transformed

a level site with remnants of a formal hotel garden into the horticultural jewel it is today. Accountant Reginald M. Faletti and lawyer Francis Price (succeeded by Robert M. Jones when Price died in 1976) were Alice Keck Park's most trusted advisors and the trustees who oversaw development of the park for the originally anonymous donor. All were actively involved in civic affairs and served on the boards of numerous nonprofit organizations, including the Museum of Art and Cottage Hospital. Almost certainly, Reginald was the behind-the-scenes catalyst whose suggestion resulted in Mrs. Park's decision to purchase the land.

I, too, had an early connection with the park; through my husband, I was privileged to witness the design process from the very beginning, to watch the garden's creation from conception to birth. I saw Grant's rough penciled sketches of paths and dry stony creeks, a pond and a hill where no feature had existed before. He drew sketches of how the park would look in five years, ten years, twenty years. And despite changes, the overall design and concept remain intact.

Now Alice Keck Park's gift can work its magic on us all. It enables us to understand the phases of our lives as stages on a journey, as part of a bigger plan that is played out each day in the rising and setting sun, and year after year in the seasons. Unconsciously we are reminded, even if only for a few moments, of the natural flow of life as a passage that carries us on the stream from birth to death. Just as sunshine follows rain and spring follows winter, plants that fade to bloom again the next season brings comfort and hope. This is the legacy of "Alice."

Elizabeth de Forest, Reginald Faletti, Francis Price. (Top to bottom).

before the garden

*T*he *4.6 acre property* that is now the Alice Keck Park Memorial Garden—bordered by Santa Barbara, Micheltorena, Garden, and Arrellaga Streets—has a rich and varied history. Before the garden, there was an experimental urban farm on the land, before the farm came a hotel, and before the hotel a gracious home. Twice the site escaped disaster in the guise of a high-rise building. Clearly fate or karma played a role in the outcome; indeed, the tradition of beautiful gardens and a reverence for the land began here long before Alice Keck Park made her anonymous gift.

Centuries before the Spanish arrived, hundreds of Chumash villages dotted the region; the entire city of Santa Barbara was carved out of what had once been that tribe's territory. However, by the time the Spanish established the Royal Presidio in 1782 and Father Junípero Serra founded the mission of Santa Barbara, the Chumash with their deep veneration for the land and sea, had retreated from the center of the city and migrated to the foothills.

Even the scattered
*   boulders below*

have a history,
*   are going somewhere*

if rather slowly,
*   resting a while*

like you and I in the
*   midst of our journey*

who stand in this
*   same place together.*

BARRY SPACKS

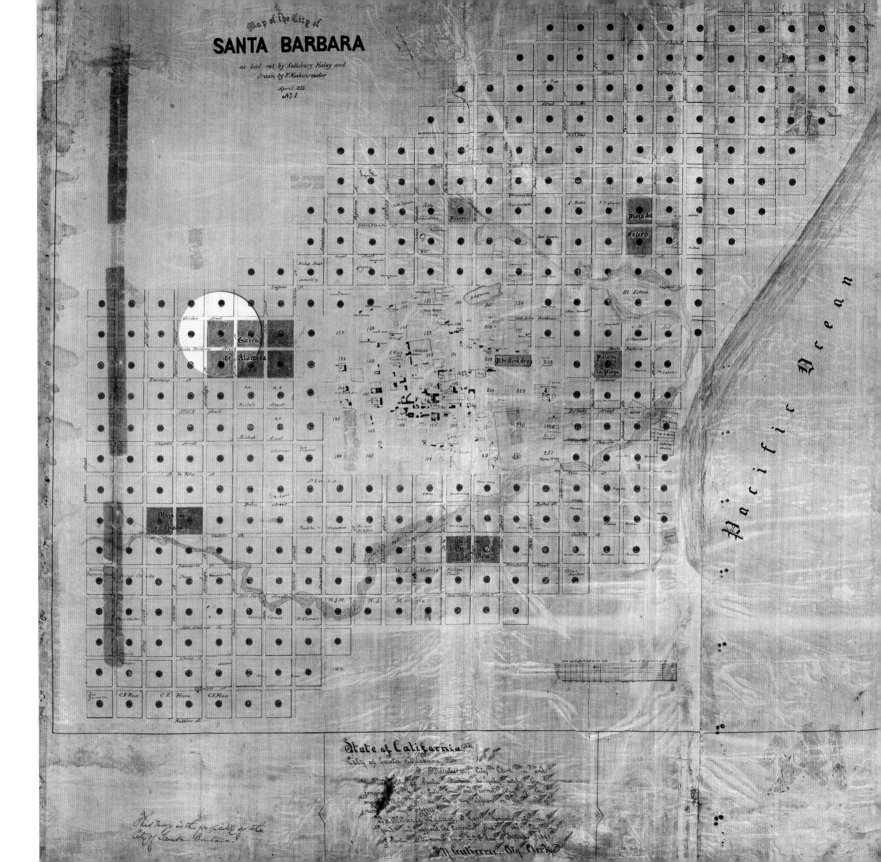

The 1853 Haley and Wackenreuder map. Alice Keck Park Memorial Garden occupies one of the six blocks designated for park use.

As a public garden, the site returns to the original intent of the founders of Santa Barbara. In 1853, three years after California became a state, the city fathers designated six blocks as the "Garden de Alameda," according to an early map. After that, the property changed hands numerous times but remained vacant until Mrs. Christian L. Herter purchased it in 1904.

ENTER THE HERTERS

Mary Miles Herter was the widow of a founding partner of Herter Brothers, a renowned furniture and interior design firm in New York. In 1882 Christian Herter had walked away from success, leaving his wife and two sons in the United States while he moved to Paris to study painting. A year later, at age 44, the man who had been described as "society's darling as well as its decorator" died of tuberculosis in the French capital.

Two decades later Mrs. Herter commissioned the prominent New York architectural firm of Delano and Aldrich to build a home in Santa Barbara. Photographs of the mansion show an elegant,

spread-out house with arched windows under a red tile roof with wide overhangs; two-story loggias on either end were wrapped around a central section to form a beautifully landscaped courtyard that featured a pool and fountain crafted from brilliantly colored, imported tile. The home, built of brick and

stone with plastered exterior walls, graced the south side of the property, for which the magnificent Santa Ynez mountain range formed a constantly changing backdrop.

EL MIRASOL

Mary Herter died in 1913, and she bequeathed the property to her only surviving son, Albert. In 1909 he and his wife, Adele, had come to Santa Barbara to help Mary decorate her newly completed mansion. After her death, the couple transformed the fine Santa Barbara home into an even lovelier hotel. They added bungalows with verandas arched by lattice pergolas, and offered five-room-three-bath and four-room-two-bath floor plans. "The grounds became a botanical masterpiece with extensive gardens and rare plants," wrote one critic of the day.

Mary Miles Herter (left) purchased the entire block in 1904 and commissioned a magnificent home, the predecessor to the El Mirasol Hotel shown in a 1929 postcard (above).

Inside the courtyard of the El Mirasol Hotel (at left). The lobby, (at right) featured magnificent rugs, furnishings, and tapestries from the Herter looms.

For their hotel Albert and Adele held a public naming contest and selected "El Mirasol," which means "the sunflower," from more than a hundred entries. In her well-documented history, "El Mirasol: From Swan to Albatross," Hattie Beresford wrote that Adele papered the drawing room with silver foil taken from Chinese tea packages, ironing each square herself. Frank Lloyd Wright described it as "the most beautiful wall covering in the world." Sadly the furnishings were lost when the building was demolished years later.

In 1920 Albert and Adele Herter sold El Mirasol to Frederick C. Clift, owner of San Francisco's Clift Hotel and the Biltmore Hotel (now The Four Seasons) in Santa Barbara. The new owner continued the tradition of lodging the rich and famous. But in 1940 the hotel was sold, and over the next twenty years ownership changed hands several more times.

Sky view of the El Mirasol Hotel. The Herters added vine covered bungalows along the perimeter of the property.

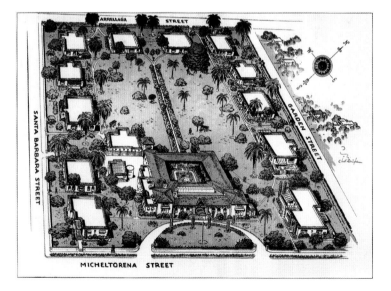

In 1962 Morgan Flagg purchased the entire property—the hotel, fifteen bungalows, and some four and a half acres—for $700,000. By now, the fifty-year-old buildings had lost their luster and required extensive maintenance. Three gardeners were also needed to maintain the elaborate landscaping. Many of the bungalows were occupied by wealthy elderly retirees who used their own furniture from previous estates. The rest of the cottages badly needed refurbishing. Muriel and Theodore Osterhaus, the resident managers of the hotel during this period, reported a series of "disastrous financial losses." Perhaps not surprisingly, in 1965 Morgan Flagg sold the hotel and land—now valued at $850,000—to Jacob Seldowitz in exchange for a ranch.

THE GLIMMER OF AN ARTS CENTER

A year later two fires destroyed the attic of the west wing of the house. Then in August 1967 Seldowitz proposed demolishing all the structures and replacing them with a nine-story, "low-rise" hotel with underground parking for 400 cars. His plan included a performing arts center that could accommodate 2,500 people. The idea of providing a cultural anchor close to the downtown area was based, in the words of project architect John Menegon, on Seldowitz's belief that "beautification alone is not enough to preserve the health of a community."

The proposal was highly controversial, however, and the development and review process included many contentious public hearings before the City Planning Commission. A small core of civic-minded residents opposed the design. Appalled at the thought of losing magnificent mountain views, fearing the dangerous precedent of allowing multi-story high-rises, and worrying that the tall structures would ruin the charm of Santa Barbara, the opposition rallied its forces…and in the end prevailed. The Planning Commission denied the zoning variance needed to develop the project. Seldowitz's response was to sell the hotel's contents and obtain a permit to raze the buildings.

TOPPLING A TOWER

Before the bulldozers could do their work, the property changed hands again. This time the site was purchased by civic and business leaders who formed the El Mirasol Investment Company and initially proposed an eleven-story condominium development. Again, a group of activists—led by Pearl Chase, who for years had worked to preserve the city's architectural character—opposed the project. Again, the battle was fierce.

At first, the City Planning Commission denied the zoning and height variance that would have been required. The developers appealed that decision to the City Council, which, on March 25,

1969, granted the variance and allowed the project to move forward. The opposition, however, did not give up. It appealed the decision, and on July 10 the court sided with Pearl Chase and her followers, ordering the City Council to rescind the variance. Nevertheless, in August 1969 bulldozers razed the site. The property now stood empty; the once gorgeous gardens were left untended. Weeds and vines grew wild, strangling magnificent trees. Thick brush and shrubs created natural shelters for the homeless. El Mirasol became known as a place to avoid, a haunted, spooky site.

EL MIRASOL CONDOMINIUM PROJECT, 87 UNITS   SANTA BARBARA

Architectural rendering of the El Mirasol Investment Company's condominiums, one of two high rise projects proposed for the site.

Besides preserving the land for today's garden, this episode had another important outcome. When a high-rise project went down to defeat for the second time, Pearl Chase was able to muster support for a referendum on an amendment to the city charter that limited all future building to just four stories. In November 1972 that amendment passed overwhelmingly. It remains in effect today.

A geodesic dome was part of the Community Environmental Council's experimental farm on the site in the early 1970s.

FARM LESSONS

After their project was defeated, the El Mirasol Investment group offered the land to the Museum of Art. The opportunity arose suddenly and required quick action by the Museum's board of directors. After a "crash" fundraising effort, led by attorney Robert M. Jones, to acquire the site, the Museum was able to secure the land by making a sizable down payment, but it lacked sufficient funds to move to the property right away. Instead, Carol Valentine, then president of the board, asked the group to allow the Community Environmental Council (CEC) to use the property for three to five years, free of charge, for an experimental urban farm. The CEC's goal was to demonstrate that agriculture "consistent and harmonious with natural cycles" should and could exist in an urban center.

Established in 1971, the El Mirasol Educational Farm was one of the earliest examples of holistic urban farming in the region; thousands of people visited, eager to learn about organic gardening techniques. Since then, of course, the concept of urban farming has spread. Many cities now sponsor allotment gardens for the public, and throughout the nation private farm cooperatives provide organic produce to their members. Certainly the visitors to the farm were enriched by their experience of the cycles of nature.

In autumn 1973 the Museum of Art board decided it no longer needed the El Mirasol site. A planned city parking lot behind its existing building would eliminate the most serious problem with the institution's State Street home. Instead, the El Mirasol property would be sold to raise funds for the Museum's renovation. The CEC tried desperately to find money to buy the property; when it was unable to do so, it recommended that the site be developed as a horticultural park. Among those who heard that suggestion were Reginald Faletti and Francis Price, Alice Keck Park's accountant and lawyer, and her two most trusted advisors. But there was no more time. Under pressure to save its investment, the Museum sold the property to the first bidder, another housing developer, and the El Mirasol farm project was dismantled.

That was not the end of the story. In 1975, when financing arrangements for the proposed condominiums fell apart, the land again reverted to the Museum. Carol Valentine remembers that the consortium threatened to default on its payments, leaving the Museum responsible for the debt and back taxes. The board was informed that "the group was prepared to walk away."

EL MIRASOL PARK

Meanwhile, out of public view, on September 28, 1975, Alice Keck Park quietly signed a trust document transferring funds to Faletti and Price to purchase the land. The trustees were to expend "all reasonable efforts to avoid any disclosure of the terms (of this trust);" the name of the donor, too, was to remain anonymous. On November 7, Faletti informed Carol Valentine of an $800,000, all-cash offer from an anonymous donor, on the condition that the land be donated to the city as a park. Her diary shows that three days later she discussed the proposed "horticultural park" with

Elizabeth de Forest of the Botanic Garden board. At first several members of the Parks Commission were opposed to the requirement of the project: like the Santa Barbara Botanic Garden, it would have to be designed as a passive horticultural garden. The commissioners wanted a more active park, perhaps even tennis courts, and argued that the city should reject the donation. But Pearl Chase and Elizabeth de Forest, along with representatives of the Botanic Garden and Museum of Art, lobbied the local government to accept both the gift and the donor's conditions.

On December 8, 1975, the City Council assented, with "no questions asked," and Price closed escrow on the purchase of Block 58, "commonly known as unimproved land referred to as 'El Mirasol' property." That document states clearly that the land was purchased with the understanding by the seller (the Santa Barbara Museum of Art) that the buyers, Faletti and Price, were purchasing the property for the "sole purpose of dedicating the property to the City of Santa Barbara for use as a free public park."

The purchase was followed in the same month by a separate agreement that conveyed the "El Mirasol Property" to the city of Santa Barbara "solely, exclusively and forever for public park purposes . . ." and added that the Trust would landscape the property and consult with representatives designated by the Botanic Garden. Finally, though the Trust would expire when construction was complete, and the city would own the park, in a noteworthy section of the document the Botanic Garden was granted an oversight role in perpetuity.

Canna × *'Erebus'* (Water Canna Lily), *Xylosma congesta* 'Compacta' (Dwarf Xylosma), *Phoenix canariensis* (Canary Island Date Palm)

a garden is born

Wisteria sinensis (Chinese Wisteria)

By *1975 the once lovely* El Mirasol property was a shambles. A jungle of overgrown shrubs and weeds buried junked cars and remnants of the Community Environmental Council's experimental urban farm, and little remained of the once-fragrant hotel garden.

Alice Keck Park had stipulated that the Santa Barbara Botanic Garden would be responsible for the development of "her" ambitious garden, and she chose Elizabeth de Forest, a member of its board of trustees, to act as her representative. In early 1975 the Botanic Garden formed a selection committee to choose a designer for what was still being called El Mirasol Park. Lila Sexton, Katherine Muller, Ralph Philbrick, John Pitman, and Elizabeth de Forest interviewed landscape architects from all over Southern California and decided on Grant Castleberg, A.S.L.A. He was chosen, de Forest told him later, because of his broad knowledge and keen interest in plant material and his innovative ideas on how to create an informal, intimate garden.

Everything in this garden –
And each plant,

Once it has found its ideal place –
Is born, grows, flowers
and bears fruit,

as if predestined to be there.

SALAH STÉTIÉ

He walked the property, observing sunlight and shadows, looking at the views and the natural contours of the place, and letting the ideas come to him gradually. Then, like an artist, he began to draw.

"I work with my hands," Castleberg says. "I sketch and the ideas come. When completed, my designs may reflect or combine influences of others—Frederick Olmstead and Thomas Church, for instance. But that happens at an unconscious level. For me, the process is like painting an abstract piece of art. In the final analysis it's painting with plants that I do, painting with an understanding of how nature will continue the process."

The only hint of the once luxurious hotel can be seen in the formal rows of Canary Island date palms (above). Grant Castleberg's small blue Porsche was a familiar site at the property (right).

Adhering to the donor's concept of a passive horticultural garden, de Forest and the rest of the committee developed broad guidelines for the landscape architect to work within. Though she herself loved native plants and landscape, de Forest insisted that their use be limited in this garden. She felt strongly that native plants require too much care and would not thrive in a public space. Dr. Ralph Philbrick, then the director of the Botanic Garden, recalls that de Forest saw the new park as an opportunity to feature striking specimens, "things that weren't the usual sixes and eights" seen elsewhere. She was interested in preserving "heritage" plants, classics that had "gone out of favor." The lovely white lilies, *Crinum ×powellii* 'Album,' in the border along Arrellaga Street were among her favorites.

Castleberg shared de Forest's and the donor's vision of the park "as a quiet space, a place of color in all seasons, a garden that would entice people to visit." For months his small blue sports car could be seen at the site, as he spent long hours getting the feel of the land.

Grant Castleberg's goal was to create a park of interest not only to horticulturists, but to ordinary people. To transform the formal structure of the hotel garden into an informal space, he removed some of the stately Canary Island date palms and broke up the rows. The remaining specimens served as focal points in the new design. Castleberg's firm developed complex planting, grading, and irrigation plans, and a water consultant was hired to work out details of the stream and pond. When the city risk manager required a four-foot fence around the water, Castleberg responded that the restriction was unacceptable. He insisted that the pond was a vital element in

Four views of the El Mirasol Hotel property show that the once lovely grounds had become an abandoned wilderness. No hint remained of the lush planting and extensive landscaping.

Phoenix canariensis (Canary Island Date Palm)

EL MIRASOL PARK

Grant Castleberg's 1975 plan (above) for what was originally known as El Mirasol Park includes designs for details (right). After she died in 1977 Alice Keck Park became known as the donor.

the park and needed to be accessible, not separated by a barrier. In his effort to salvage this critical feature, he called cities up and down the coast, checking on their experiences with pond and lake safety issues. He remembers the risk manager from Oakland joking that they sometimes fished bodies out of Lake Merritt, but that "they were all dead before they hit the water." In the end, the unfenced pond was approved.

Castleberg's plan emphasized the natural contours of the site, lowering low spots and raising higher areas. He created the pond for water lilies, koi, and ducks; laid out stony dry creeks (an idea that has since been adopted in other local landscapes); and designed intimate "rooms" separated by trees and plantings. Near the corner of Santa Barbara and Arrellaga Streets, a boardwalk meanders over a wet meadow that has been planted with white and yellow water iris. Two streams with natural sandstone boulders flow from high ground to the lower area, where the pond lies diagonally across the site. Although the plans called for feeding the streams from an existing well on the property, the well was later capped, and the park now uses city water. The diagonal water elements and the spiral mound mask all remaining traces of the earlier formal hotel garden. Only two orange trees and the double paths off Micheltorena Street serve as a reminder of the dignified entrance to El Mirasol.

Over 18 months, Castleberg spent many evenings at his drafting table at home, developing concepts and detailed planting plans. Working with his hallmark soft sketching pencil, he made broad strokes on tracing paper, creating a sheet for each season and locating plants and trees in bloom; these were layered over the base of the overall design. The original plans, labeled El Mirasol Park, still appear remarkably up-to-date twenty-five years later.

For color in various seasons, the design called for groves, each with a different kind of flowering tree. One displayed a drift of peach trees that signal the coming of spring, another a grouping of liquidamber, *Liquidambar styraciflua*, for fall foliage. Four species of coral trees, with fire-engine-red blossoms, bloom at different times of the year around the pond. West of the arbor, exotic tipu tipu trees, *Tipuana tipu*, have soft yellow blossoms and a wide canopy of foliage.

Few of the plants and trees intended for the park were generally available in 1975; many were grown specially or imported from overseas. The city Parks and Recreation Department started the coral trees and the magnificent dombeya from cuttings. The pink succulent groundcover, *Crassula multicava*, near the corner of Garden Street and Arrellaga came from Castleberg's father's house.

Most of the fixtures in the park—light posts, sundial, gazebo, pergola, and a small maintenance shed—were designed by Castleberg. Beams in the pergola were originally meant to use salvaged beams from the El Mirasol Hotel, however termite damage was too extensive so new beams were crafted as exact replicas. The sundial initially included a locally crafted wrought-iron stylus whose shadow indicated the time. Unfortunately the stylus was stolen not long after the garden opened. The black iron fence around the upper half of the park, also specially designed, was added just before the garden was completed to prevent visitors trampling bulbs and groundcover. By that time Alice Keck Park had died; her sister, Willametta Day, paid for the fence.

ALICE KECK PARK
MEMORIAL GARDEN
Landscape Architect : GRANT CASTLEBERG
General Contractor : DON GREENE, INC.
Landscape Contractor : SO. CALIF. LANDSCAPES

Preliminary sketches by Jim Hitchman, a draftsman in Castleberg's firm, illustrating features of the still-proposed design: the mound with the flowering tree at the summit, the pond, and one of the many winding paths lined with trees that are now a hallmark of the Garden.

26

Castleberg's detailed plans for two of the feature elements in the Garden. The gazebo (right) and the sundial (below). The Gazebo was designed to be built on concrete posts sunk into the pond so the structure extends over the water. This charming spot has become a focal point in the park especially for little children who can be seen peeking between posts in the railing to watch the fish in the pond and turtles on the rocks. The light fixtures on the gazebo, as well as all the lights in the park, were specially designed by Castleberg's firm and built by Old World Metalcraft in Solvang. The beams that can be seen on the gazebo are exact replicas of beams that graced the El Mirasol Hotel.

The plan for the sundial (left) reveals details often overlooked by the casual visitor. Hidden at the top of the mound, is the brick and stone mosaic that forms the sundial. Sundials were originally an attempt by man to articulate time. Still today, they continue to intrigue us. Cobblestones form the background for the "sun clock" and red bricks paint the time (roman numerals) and pointers. The stylus, which was stolen shortly after the park opened, pointed exactly to the celestial pole, or towards the North Star. While the stylus was in place the sundial proved to be very accurate.

Grant Castleberg in the still-under-construction pergola.

The plan added pathways over the low soggy areas of the site.

Vince Stumpo, Elizabeth de Forest, and Sydney Baumgartner reviewing the rock wall of the pond before it was filled.

During construction, Elizabeth de Forest could often be seen on the site along with local landscape architect Sydney Baumgartner, who was married to de Forest's nephew. Baumgartner started her career as a landscape architect working for Castleberg as a draftsman on this project; she went on to become an associate with the firm before leaving to open her own office. For a number of years Baumgartner continued her involvement as a board member at the Botanic Garden. As a member of the Alice Keck Park committee, she assumed the Botanic Garden's "oversight role." In the 1990s, when two new areas were added, she collaborated with Castleberg on the design.

In October 1979 the Santa Barbara News Press reported, "Although its formal dedication is not scheduled until Spring, the Alice Keck Park Memorial Garden is open. Already it's become a favorite haven for Santa Barbarans." Early the next year the city officially opened the park, heralding the occasion with a ribbon-cutting ceremony.

Since then the Santa Barbara City Parks and Recreation Department has been responsible for maintenance of the park. Gardens rely on their caretakers to survive; administrators for both the city and the department are to be commended for their ongoing commitment to maintaining this park as a showpiece of the city. One city employee in particular, Carol Terry, is fondly remembered for her years of on-site maintenance and loving garden care. Over the years, besides Carol, many City maintenance staff and a group of volunteers have devoted their time and talent tending the Garden and deserve thanks. Simply keeping a horticultural park in top-notch shape takes more than a public agency can afford; enhancements and replanting have had to be specially funded. Since 1980 there have been only three significant changes to the park.

WHO NEEDS WATER?

In 1993, following several years of serious drought, the Santa Barbara Public Works Department funded a Low-Water-Using Demonstration Garden at the southeast end of the garden, featuring drought-tolerant plants. The beautiful area features a dry stream bed bordered by gray and silvery foliage. Along Micheltorena Street, colorful bougainvillea nestles between orange trees, and a lush rosemary named Lockwood de Forest, *Rosmarinus officinalis* 'Lockwood de Forest' (after Elizabeth's husband), trails over the stone wall.

A FEAST FOR THE SENSES

The following year, in 1994, Elvira Broome Doolan bequeathed $50,000 to the Santa Barbara Foundation to fund a public garden for the visually impaired. The Foundation asked Jeff Cope, Assistant Parks and Recreation Department Director, to carry out the project, and he selected Alice Keck Park Memorial Garden as the site. Funded partially by Mrs. Doolan's grant and augmented by an additional $17,000 from the Santa Barbara Foundation as well as money from the Parks Department, the Sensory Garden for the visually impaired was developed. It is planted with brightly colored, highly scented, and textural plants, which allow people with only limited sight to experience the garden. Ten audio stations along the paths provide descriptions of the plants and use Braille-like markings to indicate the locations of the varieties discussed.

Virginia Hayes, a Santa Barbara horticulturist, described the Sensory Garden for the Santa Barbara Independent: "By listening to the narration at each stop, visitors are invited to explore the plant

kingdom with senses other than sight. Softly hairy, sandpapery rough, smooth and succulent leaves are described and located for anyone to reach out and touch. Scents and flowers and even foliage are identified for the visitor to experience. The sounds of falling water and happy children are used to orient the hearer in the larger landscape of the park."

The low water demonstration garden features silvery plants and a dry creek bed.

It's a constantly changing, inspirational scene, as Virginia Hayes wrote in March 2005: "When I want to see what's going on in the floral world, one of the first places I go is Alice Keck Park Memorial Garden…. I made my yearly pilgrimage to stand under the massive Dombeya the other day. Not only could I look up into thousands of dainty rose-colored bells adorning the branches above, I stood in a carpet of the same flowers that obliterated the muddy path below."

Although "Alice" is celebrating her silver anniversary, in "park-life years" she is still very young. Even the landscape architect never dreamed the garden would be as popular as it is, and the large number of visitors puts a burden on the landscape. The Parks Department has diligently attended to its maintenance, but additional funds are always needed. To truly sustain the garden as Alice Keck Park would have wished, an endowment fund should augment the city maintenance budget.

In the Sensory Garden visually handicapped visitors enjoy the texture of a leaf (above) and brightly colored plants. Ten audio posts provide descriptions of plants and guides to their locations (upper right). The park is part of the city's pesticide free program (right).

A decade later, in 2004, the city of Santa Barbara adopted an integrated pest management strategy to eliminate pesticide use in public areas. Alice Keck Park Memorial Garden was designated as a Pesticide Free Zone and serves as a demonstration garden for the use of alternatives to pesticides and sustainable landscaping practices.

In 2005, after twenty-five years, "Alice" remains immensely popular. Like the Velveteen Rabbit in the famed children's story, the park has developed bare spots reflecting both the wear and tear of use and the natural ravages of time. Yet undoubtedly Castleberg's goal of designing a park that appeals to people of all ages has been achieved. Visitors to the park see toddlers entranced by enormous fish in the pond, lovers holding hands, business people eating lunch, elderly ladies and gentlemen strolling with walkers. There are frequently musicians performing on the lawn, poetry readings, weddings, and memorial services.

Yet such details pale when you consider the effect of "Alice." A park is never really completed; it is a work in progress, a living organism. Plants will die and be replaced, paths will wash out, rain and wind and heat will take their toll. Like any living organism a park requires constant care. Only one thing never changes: the delight it produces never disappears.

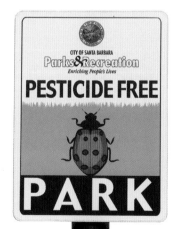

Tabebuia chrysotricha (Golden Trumpet Tree)

Iris pseudacorus (Yellow Flag Iris)

*It is a wholesome and necessary thing for us to turn again to the earth and
in the contemplation of her beauties to know of wonder and humility.*

RACHEL CARSON

spring

Above: Wisteria sinensis (Chinese Wisteria). *Facing page: Tagetes lemmonii* (Bush Marigold, Copper Canyon Daisy), *Psoralea pinnata* (Blue Pea, Scurfey Pea)

We cannot fathom the mystery of a single flower. Nor is it intended that we should.

JOHN RUSKIN

Above: Babiana stricta (Baboon Flower), *Limonium perezii* (Sea Lavender, Statice). *Facing page: Pelargonium tomentosum* (Peppermint Geranium)

*Every flower
is a soul blossoming
in Nature.*

GERARD DE NERVAL

Old Tree –
How exquisite the white blossom
On the gnarled branch!
Thickened trunk, erratic shape
Battered by winter winds,
Bent in the long cold.

Young ones may please
The aesthete,
But old trees –
The miracle of their flowering
Against such odds –
Bring healing.

MAY SARTON

Facing page: Leptospermum laevigatum (Australian Tea Tree) *flower. Above: Leptospermum laevigatum* (Australian Tea Tree)

This is the place where you can simply experience and bring forth what you are and what you might be. At first you may find nothing happens there. But if you have a sacred place and use it, something will eventually happen.

JOSEPH CAMBELL

Facing page: Toona sinensis 'Flamingo' *{Cedrela sinensis}* (Cigar Box Tree). *Above: Helictotrichon sempervirens* (Blue Oat Grass), *Alstroemeria psittacina* (Peruvian Lily), *Ceiba speciosa {Chorisia speciosa}* (Floss Silk Tree)

Clivia miniata 'Belgian Hybrid' (Kaffir Lily), *Rosa* 'Mme. Alfred Carrier'

The air provides:
it feeds the breath.

There is no sun that
lacks for light.

Blind blossoms can't
see their colors glow.

In unwillable ways
we are beautiful.

BARRY SPACKS

Tabebuia chrysotricha (Golden Trumpet Tree)

Erythrina coralloides (African Coral Tree), *Acanthus mollis* (Bear's Breeches)

One touch of nature...makes all the world kin.

WILLIAM SHAKESPEARE

Cotoneaster salicifolia 'Herbstfeuer' (Willow-Leaf Cotoneaster), *Tropaeolum majus* (Nasturtium), *Dietes vegeta [Moraea iridioides]* (Fortnight Lily)

Irises on their stalks
Gently bend before the breeze,
Bordering the walks.

SHŌSUN

Iris orientalis [I. ochroleuca] (Yellow Band Iris)

Aristea ecklonii (Blue Stars)

Aquilegia formosa (Western Columbine), *Aristea ecklonii* (Blue Stars), *Iris 'Nada'* (Butterfly Iris),
Dietes vegeta [Moraea iridioides] (Fortnight Lily), *Cistus* 'Sunset' (Rockrose), *Clivia miniata* 'Belgian Hybrid' (Kaffir Lily)

I go among trees
     and sit still.

All my stirring
     becomes quiet

around me like
     circles on water.

My tasks lie in
     their places

where I left them,
     asleep like cattle.

WENDELL BERRY

Jacaranda mimosifolia (Jacaranda)

Ceiba insignis [Chorisia insignis] (White Flowering Floss Silk Tree)

Thunbergia gregorii [T. gibsonii] (Orange Clock Vine)

summer

When we pay attention to nature's music, we find that everything on the earth contributes to its harmony.

HAZRAT INAYAT KHAN

We do not inherit the world from our ancestors, we borrow it from our children.

NATIVE AMERICAN WISDOM

Dianella tasmanica (Flax Lily)

*We must
learn
to see
the world
anew.*

ALBERT EINSTEIN

Romneya coulteri (Matilija Poppy)

Crinum ×*powellii* 'Album' (Crinum Lily), *Hypericum* 'Rowallane' (St. Johnswort)

Facing page: Hemerocallis hybrids (Daylily), Zephyranthes candida (Fairy Lily, Zephyr Flower, Rain Lily). Above: Miscanthus sinensis (Maiden Grass)

Above: Acanthus mollis (Bear's Breeches), *Erythrina falcata* (Brazilian Coral Tree). *Facing page: Corymbia ficifolia* [*Eucalyptus ficifolia*] (Red Flowering Gum)

Corymbia ficifolia [Eucalyptus ficifolia] (Red Flowering Gum)

All is dance: the sun glides along the horizon;
now the leaves sway; now the earth spins.

DAVID IGNATOW

So many gods, so many creeds,
So many paths that wind and wind,
While just the art of being kind
Is all the sad world needs.

ELLA WHEELER WILCOX

Facing page: Agapanthus orientalis hybrids (Lily-Of-The-Nile). *Above: Hedychium gardnerianum* (Kahili Ginger), *Tibouchina urvilleana* (Princess Flower),
Agapanthus orientalis hybrids (Lily-Of-The-Nile), *Hibiscus rosa-sinensis* 'White Wings' (Hibiscus), *Pontederia cordata* (Azure Pickerel Weed), *Centaurea gymnocarpa* (Dusty Miller)

We have to get quiet.
We have to be still, and
that's harder and
harder in this century.

JANE KENYON

Nymphaea hybrid (Waterlily)

In an oasis of grace
Rest, rejoice, and rejuvenate
Pause a while.

Paul Castleberg

Facing page: Tipuana tipu (Tipu Tree). *Above: Canna × 'Ra'* (Water Canna Lily), *Tecoma stans [Stenolobium stans]* (Yellow Elder, Yellow Trumpet Flower), *Clematis lasiantha* (Pipestems)

Pistacia chinensis (Chinese Pistache)

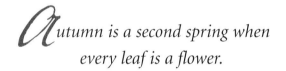

*utumn is a second spring when
every leaf is a flower.*

ALBERT CAMUS

One leaf left on a branch and
not a sound of sadness or despair.
One leaf left on a branch and
no unhappiness.
One leaf all by itself in the air
and it does not speak of
loneliness or death.
One leaf and it spends itself in
swaying mildly in the breeze.

DAVID IGNATOW

Liquidambar styraciflua (American Sweetgum)

Centranthus ruber (Red Valerian)

Kniphofia hybrid (Red Hot Poker, Torch Lily), *Hibiscus rosa-sinensis* 'Ross Estey' (Hibiscus), *Penstemon* hybrid (Garden Penstemon), *Bougainvillea spectabilis* 'Rosenka' (Bougainvillea 'Rosenka'), *Anemone ×hybrida [A. japonica]* (Japanese Anemone, Windflower), *Amaryllis belladonna [Brunsvigia rosea]* (Naked Lady)

Pelargonium hybrid (Scented Geranium), *Tecoma* × *smithii* (Orange Bells)

The most beautiful thing we can experience is the mysterious. It is the source of all true art and all science. He to whom this emotion is a stranger, who can no longer pause to wonder and stand rapt in awe, is as good as dead: his eyes are closed.

ALBERT EINSTEIN

Golden fish in the peaceful pond
mask the truth,
beneath still water
nothing is quiet.

ANNE-MARIE CASTLEBERG

I wish I understood the beauty in leaves falling.

To whom are we beautiful as we go?

DAVID IGNATOW

Facing page: Liquidambar styraciflua (American Sweetgum). *Above: Prunus campanulata* (Taiwan Flowering Cherry)

Facing page: Cuphea micropetala. Above: Brugmansia hybrid [Datura hybrid] (Angel's Trumpet), *Canna* × *'Erebus'* (Water Canna Lily)

Salix matsudana "Tortuosa" (Corkscrew Willow, Dragon Claw Willow)

winter

*It is all rich farewell now to leaves, to color. I think of the
trees and how simply they let go, let fall the riches of a
season, how without grief (it seems) they can let go and go
deep into their roots for renewal and sleep.*

MAY SARTON

Dombeya cacuminum (Strawberry Snowball Tree)

Facing page: Bauhinia ×blakeana (Hong Kong Orchid Tree). *Above, right: Nymphaea* hybrid (Waterlily), *Aeonium hybrid* (Aeonium)

The goal of life is living in

agreement with nature.

Zeno

Pyrus kawakamii (Evergreen Pear)

Magnolia × *soulangeana* (Saucer Magnolia)

The real voyage
of discovery
consists not in
seeking new
landscapes
but in having
new eyes.

MARCEL PROUST

Pelargonium cordifolium [P. cordatum] (Heart-leaf Geranium), *Narcissus* hybrid (Daffodil), *Loropetalum chinense* hybrid (Fringe Flower),
Narcissus hybrid (Narcissus), *Magnolia* ×*soulangeana* (Saucer Magnolia), *Senna didymobotrya [Cassia nairobensis]* (Cassia)

Hyacinthoides hispanica [Scilla hispanica, Scilla campanulata] (Spanish Bluebell)

Alone on a bench
blue sky above
a thousand blossoms bring
psychic nourishment
in the middle of the day.

TANA SOMMER

Prunus campanulata (Taiwan Flowering Cherry)

Arbutus 'Marina' (Strawberry Tree), *Prunus campanulata* (Taiwan Flowering Cherry), *Leucojum aestivum* (Summer Snowflake)

Archontophoenix cunninghamiana [Seaforthia elegans] (King Palm), *Brahea armata* (Mexican Blue Palm)

Phoenix canariensis (Canary Island Date Palm), *Phoenix reclinata* (Senegal Date Palm), *Euphorbia characias* ssp. *wulfenii*

Above: Fatsia japonica [Aralia seiboldii, A. japonica] (Japanese Aralia), Elegia capensis (Horsetail Restio). Facing page: Aloe striata (Coral Aloe)

who was alice?

Prunus campanulata (Taiwan Flowering Cherry)

B orn on May 12, 1918, Alice Keck Park lived a privileged yet eccentric life marred by tragic events. She died on June 24, 1977, at just fifty-nine, rumored to be living in a trailer outside Tucson with only her two lhasa apso dogs for company. In a mix-up reminiscent of a grand opera plot, her Italian common-law husband continued writing her love letters years after they'd parted, letters she never received. One telegram—"Happy Santa Barbara's Day, thinking of you always"—arrived six months after her death, setting off a bizarre legal case that has its unsolved mysteries to this day. Another mystery is why Alice, who only lived in Santa Barbara for a short time, chose to leave her entire estate to organizations there. Could it be that is where she spent her happiest years?

Those who contemplate the beauty of the earth find reserves of strength that will endure as long as life lasts. … There is something infinitely healing in the repeated refrains of nature – the assurance that dawn comes after night, and spring after winter.

RACHEL CARSON

Little-known and reclusive, Alice was a member of the famous philanthropic Keck family. Today, the Keck Foundation holds assets of close to a billion dollars, and its name is connected to many prestigious institutions: Cal Tech, Stanford University, Keck School of Medicine at the University of Southern California, and the Keck Observatory in Hawaii, to name just a few. While the Keck Foundation's goal is to fund far-reaching projects for the benefits of humanity, its focus is on science, engineering, and medicine. Alice, though, chose to give a horticultural garden to the people of Santa Barbara—a striking contrast to her family's emphasis on technology.

Alice Bertha Keck's father founded the immensely successful Superior Oil Company. A self-made man, William Myron Keck, Sr., had attended school only through the sixth grade. In the early 1900s he moved from Pennsylvania to California and worked in the oil fields around Coalinga. It was there he met and married a Canadian nurse, Alice Bertha, whose youngest daughter would share her name.

William Keck was fascinated by the drilling process and perfected new rotary techniques that revolutionized the oil industry. Intelligent, energetic, and fiercely independent, he was determined to succeed. And succeed he did. At one time, Superior was the most expensive stock listed on the New York Stock Exchange. The family moved to oil-rich Trinidad for a few years; two of their six children were born there. Later, they returned to California and purchased a home in Alhambra. Then, in 1923, Keck bought a large home in Pasadena and a Pierce Arrow limousine, for which he hired two chauffeurs.

Alice (above) at Santa Barbara Girls School in 1932, also attended by her sister, Willametta, nicknamed Willie. Willie on the left and Alice on the right in the group photo, (right).

GROWING UP

The Keck family spent many summers in Montecito. Alice attended Santa Barbara Girls School for just one year—she completed her education in Washington, D.C.—but her sister, Willametta, remained to finish high school. Heartie Anne Look, a school friend, recalls Alice as a "vivacious, red-haired girl, a lot of fun." Joanna Bard Newton and Jane Rich Mueller, who were also classmates, remember Alice differently, as shy, embarrassed about her weight, and intensely aware she wasn't as pretty as her sister or her mother.

Despite her economic advantages, Alice was familiar with catastrophe. Two of her siblings had died young, and her mother was killed in a puzzling car crash when Alice, the last person to see her mother alive, was eighteen. "Following one of the most mysterious accidents ever to be investigated by Pasadena police," the newspapers reported, "on August 19, 1936 Alice Bertha Keck, wife of William M. Keck… died in the Huntington Memorial Hospital about two hours after she had been thrown from a new automobile in which she was driving alone."

After that, during the 1940s, the family purchased the 2,500-acre Curtis Hutton Ranch in Santa Ynez, and Alice, who delighted in the natural landscape, spent much of her time there. A friend from that time described the young heiress as "mad about animals"; on the ranch she could enjoy the dogs and horses.

MARRIAGE

In 1953, Alice married David Park, a handsome Santa Barbara socialite, son of the Parks of Park Lane in Montecito. David attended Cate School and later worked for Pan American Airlines. He is remembered by friends as "a delightful fellow." David was an accomplished horseman who enjoyed playing polo, hunting, and fishing. Even then Alice shunned publicity, so she and David eloped to Paris. Alice called her father to tell him of her marriage, saying

AMONG THOSE PRESENT — When Miss Alice Keck, daughter of William Keck of Los Angeles... Park of Santa Barbara rode to their wedding in Paris

the only witness had been a "Newfie," her Newfoundland dog named Decoy. Adolphus Andrews, David Park's roommate at both Cate and Princeton, recalls that at the time of the wedding, "there was a

widely published photograph of the two of them leaving the Ritz by car, with one of Alice's huge dogs behind them."

David and Alice set up housekeeping in Montecito in a gracious home at 1895 East Valley Road, near the Valley Club. Located on three acres, the main house was designed for the original owners by Mary Craig; it centered around an atrium with a pebbled mosaic floor. The gardens, said to be "glorious, with reflecting pools and an enchanting orchard," were the work of noted landscape architect Thomas Church. A guest house, a large swimming pool, and a "Greek Theatre" also graced the property.

According to people who knew them, the couple was happily married. Shelly Ruston, whose sister was married to David Park's brother, remembers that Alice was deeply in love with David.

The gracious Montecito home (above) of Alice and David Park. Shown left, Alice and David and Alice's "Newfie" dog in Paris where they were married in 1953.

David Park(above) and Alice (right) in 1955. David died just one year later.

Another friend says that Alice "slimmed down and looked attractive," and that even though she was "intensely quiet, a shy private person, quite different from her sister, Willametta, she and David entertained often." David was described as a "Renaissance Man," attractive and interested in many things. Alice's life during those years focused on music, the arts, and travel. A "noted hostess and benefactor for many causes," she was involved with the Botanic Garden and a member of the Museum of Art board of trustees.

In June 1956, after only three years of marriage, David Park died, leaving Alice childless and devastated. David Myrick, a local historian and childhood friend of the Park family, suggests that the death was related to David's severe asthma, which he had suffered since childhood. Regardless of the cause, her husband's passing sent Alice into a tailspin. She began drinking heavily, and in 1959 she sold her home and most of its fine furnishings. Worried for Alice's health, Willametta convinced her sister to get away to Europe and arranged for a nurse-companion to accompany her.

In the early 1960s Alice purchased a villa near Como in Northern Italy and traveled extensively in France and Switzerland; she studied Italian and French, but she continued to drink excessively. The nurse-companion returned to the United States alone, reportedly after checking Alice into a sanitarium near Milan.

A Life Abroad

While in the sanitarium in 1962, Alice took Italian lessons from Bruno Valentino Silvio Leonarduzzi, an Italian war veteran. Born in Verona on April 27, 1920, Bruno was two years younger than Alice and, like her, was short and chubby. He had studied a wide range of subjects in Italy and abroad—psychology, philosophy, classical studies—and had trained as a counselor and physical education teacher. He spoke Greek, Italian, French, and Latin, and a lawyer who met him years later characterized him as a "Don Quixote" character.

During World War II Bruno had been wounded in the head in the decisive desert battle of El Alamein. The war injury would affect him throughout his life, leaving him with a short attention span and a nervous, highly emotional disposition. Bruno's role in Alice's story really only came to light years later, during the protracted legal battle over her will. In 1979, he gave an extensive deposition about their relationship, in the Milan law offices of Marino Bastianini. After that, other attorneys came to know him, including Brian Rapp, who found him like a child but "very believable. His honesty and integrity are beyond question. Everything he has ever said checked out, and he was very much in love with Alice."

At the time he met Alice, Bruno was teaching physical education at the Instituto Canizzaro at Rho. "Mutual friends, who were aware of her problems (she was then in a clinic in Como for a disintoxication program from alcoholism) and my qualifications … introduced me to her," he said in 1979, "recommending me as teacher for the Italian language, hoping that at the same time I could be of help to her for the other problem." Savoring life, he tried to encourage Alice to do the same, urging her to "rediscover her various interests, helping her to regain a better psychological and physical equilibrium."

Over the next few years Alice grew to trust Bruno, despite her fear of publicity and her always-on-the-move lifestyle. Before agreeing to meet him, she had actually had the Italian vetted by the local police.

Experiences, imagined or real, had left Alice deathly afraid not only of strangers, but also of those close to her, including some members of her family. Her fears frequently verged on paranoia, although a bitter proxy fight that took place after her death—between her brother and Willametta—suggests that Alice may have had legitimate reasons for concern.

When Willam Keck died in 1964, leadership of Superior Oil fell to one of his surviving sons, Howard. Alice and her sister were often at odds with their brothers; Alice feared that they were trying to wrest control of her company shares. After she died, in fact, Howard Keck opposed a sale of Superior Oil to Mobil, while Willametta, who was in favor of the deal, took out newspaper ads advising shareholders to vote a resolution that would permit it. On September 28, 1984, the sale went through: Mobil bought Superior Oil for $5.7 billion, further enriching the Keck heirs, who owned 22.6 percent of the company stock, and making Willametta one of the 400 wealthiest women in America, according to Forbes magazine.

A New Relationship

For several years Bruno and Alice remained platonic friends. He visited her three or four times each month, for several days at a time, always staying in separate rooms. "Mrs. Keck Park put at my disposal a room in the villa in Como in Via Cardano 6," Bruno said, "for when we were up late at night, as her habits were quite irregular."

She also arranged a room for him when she moved to a hotel. At one point she quarreled with the custodian at her villa, and after slapping the man across the face, "she decided to abandon the villa abruptly to go to Switzerland, at first to Lugano and later to

Locarno, where she stayed at Hotel La Palma." The formality of their relationship was noticed by the concierge there; Giuseppe Bass said he "never saw Mrs. Park and Mr. Leonarduzzi hold hands or display affection toward one another in any other manner, nor did I ever hear either of them address any term of endearment to the other." Throughout this period Bruno continued to teach at the school in

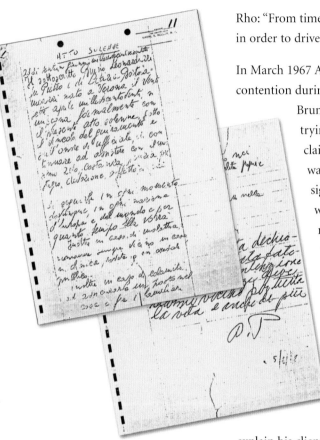

The secret, sacred pact Alice and Bruno signed in 1968.

Rho: "From time to time, Mrs. Park would wait for me at the school, in order to drive me to the Hotel La Palma at the end of my lessons."

In March 1967 Alice signed a will that would become a matter of contention during the probate of her estate, since it did not mention Bruno. Lawyers for the charities named in the document, trying hard to preserve their clients' hefty bequests, claimed the omission was deliberate. The legal issue was this: If Alice and Bruno were married before she signed the will, or were likely to marry, the oversight would be considered intentional, and Bruno would not be entitled to any of the estate. However, that was not the case. Bruno later clarified the sequence of events. Before March 1967, he said, "our relationship was not characterized by the particular affection that was manifested one year later, on February 3rd, 1968, when in our privacy we stipulated the 'secret, sacred pact.'"

Indeed, by 1968, things had changed. Love entered the relationship. Years later Bruno's Italian lawyer, Marino Bastianini, tried to explain his client's feeling, saying Bruno and Alice considered their love "so noble that it can't be talked about, it must be kept secret." They did pledge their faith to each other, though, in a "secret, sacred" pact. Handwritten in Italian by Bruno, the document was signed by both of them on February 3. The first section states:

Being my father, Pietro Leonarduzzi, and my mother, Leticia Bortolameazzi, born in Verona on April 27, 1920. I formally undertake with a present solemn deed under oath and on my honor as an officer

in the Army to continue to assist with the maximum zeal, constancy, capability, prestige, devotion and affection to follow her (Alice) in any moment, anywhere in any nation of Europe and the world and for how long she will want. Moreover, in case of illness, I will take to remain always close to her in the house, in the clinic, in a private clinic or in a public house. Moreover, in case of calamity, I undertake to insure her a place in the house and within my family, being it understood within the limits of economical possibilities of myself and of my relatives. Luzerne, January 21, 1968.

Alice added, in her own writing:

As the present declaration has been made with the idea and the intention that Leonarduzzi must stay close to me for the rest of his life, and even beyond this point. Signed "AP"

Did she mean for eternity? That is certainly what the pact suggests. "For the rest of his life, and even beyond…"—those words would haunt Bruno, and after her death he vowed to dedicate himself to her memory.

Alice now wore a wedding ring and introduced herself to everyone as Alice Leonarduzzi. She and Bruno considered themselves man and wife, and he confirmed that the marriage had been consummated. Alice used her husband's name in correspondence, too. On September 25, 1969, she wrote to Dr. Katherine Muller, Director of the Botanic Garden in Santa Barbara, and signed the letter Alice B. Leonarduzzi (Formerly Mrs. David Park). A plaque in the library of the Botanic Garden still commemorates a donation from Mrs. Alice Leonarduzzi. Meanwhile, the rhythm and fabric of the couple's lives changed drastically. Bruno gave up his teaching job and traveled everywhere with Alice. But even with him at her side, she was reluctant to stay in one place for long. They were constantly on the move.

"From Switzerland we went to France on the Cote d'Azur and then to London," Bruno remembered. "We were continuing together the type of life that was to be our life in the future. We were traveling around and I was satisfying all her desires remaining constantly with her." Suddenly Alice decided that she wanted to go back to the United States. The couple left London and arrived in Seattle in February 1969.

It was there that Alice told Bruno about a Colorado law that would allow them to get married "without publicity (one of the things that she hated more than anything else in the world) that a ceremony civil or religious would have provided. It was well known how she loved privacy; only I was allowed to take pictures of her and to paint a portrait of her."

According to Bruno, sometimes not even her accountant, Reginald Faletti, knew where they were staying. "Once Mr. Faletti sent a telegram to my brother in Milan to find out where we were, while we were just very close to Santa Barbara," Bruno said.

Alice remained on strained terms with many who had been close to her. Bruno pointed to one incident in Arizona as an example: They were in the hotel of the Grand Canyon, he said, "and in the course of a folkloristic show of Indian dance outdoors, Alice recognized among the guests her mother-in-law, mother of her deceased husband David; and she shook me by an arm and dragged me away, and once she got the confirmation from the concierge of the hotel that it was

Brugmansia hybrids *[Datura hybrids]* (Angel's Trumpet), *Clivia miniata* 'Belgian Hybrid' (Kaffir Lily)

indeed her mother-in-law she wanted to leave immediately." He said it was "as though she had seen the devil in person. (We took a cab and then a private plane and left.)"

Alice's fear of being seen by her mother-in-law was symptomatic of her severe paranoia, in fact she liked her mother-in-law and even remembered her in her will years after David's death. Alice was equally difficult when it came to hotels. She insisted on visiting many and then became very selective about choosing the one she liked; often her reasons were irrational, almost superstitious. On one occasion an exhausted Bruno wanted to settle on a place so they could finally sit down. Alice demanded that they continue, however. She wanted things the way she wanted them.

Bruno confessed that he would "have really liked to slap her at those moments for her Latin, Latin character." Another time, when they were visiting Tucson, Alice wanted to stay at the Pioneer Hotel, but after spending hours inspecting room after room, she rejected them all. The one suite she wanted was occupied. She drove everyone crazy, he said. They ended up going elsewhere until the apartment she desired at the Pioneer became vacant. Three days after moving in, Alice got into an argument with the hotel management, she claimed they didn't listen to her or do what she wanted. "Away," Alice commanded Bruno. And the couple moved on.

In retrospect, Bruno described her sensitivity as almost a sixth sense. One rationale Alice gave for their abrupt departure was the danger of fire; the possibility terrified her. As it happened, only months after they left the Pioneer, there was an awful blaze. It was as though she had intuited the danger long before the fact.

Bruno and Alice remained in the United States for roughly five years, much of that in Colorado, "which we consider as our home, for both the fact of the common law marriage and for the panorama that Alice liked very much." They also continued their travels around the country—touching down in California, Tucson, Salt Lake City, and Hawaii. Wherever they went, though, they listed their permanent residence as Colorado, and they kept a post office box there, where all their "correspondence was sent together with two local newspapers, the Colorado Today and the Aspen Times, and an Italian newspaper."

As Bruno and Alice Leonarduzzi they even bought a house in Colorado, in a town called Rifle, and they planned to move there until a problem arose. Bruno remembered, "The people who were living in it at that time would not vacate it, so after some time it was decided to resell it."

Their lifestyle may have seemed strange, but it was evidently satisfying. "Alice had various interests and curiosities," he said, "mostly regarding nature, that she wanted to fulfill at any cost, and I was making her happy in all her desires even if that would cost me sacrifice."

During this period, Bruno taught advanced conversational French classes in a local school, and he attended public first aid courses. Together the pair entertained and participated in the life of their community. "We would also get up at 5 a.m. to study the songs of birds, we went mountain climbing, went for long walks and fishing (one of the favorite hobbies of Alice). Alice wanted me to paint a landscape and some flowers she particularly liked in oil paint or drawings that she wanted to keep for herself."

Bruno also went back and forth to Europe—"I made approximately nineteen trips," he said—to shop for something special or to take care of other business on Alice's behalf. He was adamant that he never acted with a thought to her inheritance. "One hundred percent of my time was devoted to Alice. My disinterest for money was total." Even the funds she put at his disposal "were used by me for our mutual expenses and thereafter were never touched."

By spring 1973 Alice was restless again and eager to return to Italy. "We arrived in Milan and then we went to Tuscany," Bruno said, "where Alice wanted to study the Etruscan civilization that I had many times studied with her. We went to Livorno, Florence, and many times visited the Etruscan Museum of Volterra."

*A bird disturbs
no more than one twig
of the green leaved
peach tree.*

WILLIAM CARLOS WILLIAMS

IN GRATEFUL MEMORY OF
ALICE KECK PARK
1918 - 1977
WHOSE GENEROSITY AND LOVE OF
SANTA BARBARA HAVE CREATED THIS PARK
UNDER THE DIRECTION OF
ELIZABETH DE FOREST
AND
THE SANTA BARBARA BOTANIC GARDEN
AND THE DESIGN OF GRANT CASTLEBERY A.S.L.A.
REGINALD M. FALETTI AND FRANCIS PRICE TRUSTEES
1979

The bronze plaque in the wall of the rotunda acknowledges Alice's generosity and those responsible for creating the park.

BACK TO AMERICA

Then, on December 4 Alice decided to return to the States. This time she would go alone. Bruno's mother was ill, and he was unwilling to leave her. "My mother… was getting much worse; she finally became totally blind because of diabetes. In fact she died a few days later on December 27."

The social situation in Italy may have contributed to Alice's decision. She may even have feared personal harm. Earlier in the year young John Paul Getty, grandson of multi-billionaire oil tycoon J. Paul Getty, had been kidnapped in Rome. His grandfather refused to pay the $3 million ransom until one of the boy's ears was cut off and sent to a newspaper. That event, plus general political unrest in the country, fueled Alice's distrust and led to her impetuous, almost rageful departure.

Bruno insisted Alice didn't leave Italy to get away from him; she wasn't angry with him. But clearly her behavior had became progressively more erratic. In several arguments she slapped people across the face. Marino Bastianini explained, "Just before leaving to go back to the States, she was quarreling very often with everybody here in Italy. She had an argument with a cook in a restaurant, and an argument with a waiter. She had the bottle of wine go back and refused the bottle because it was bad three or four times, and she was very nervous about things in Italy."

She had done something similar in Switzerland, he added, and slapped her financial manager in Como. Even after she returned to America, she told her lawyer and accountant she had gotten into an argument with a someone in Milan: "She had gone to the apartment of a woman and slapped her across the face. After slapping the woman, Alice told them she got into a cab and left Italy and never returned."

After Alice's departure, Bruno had no further contact with her, but he continued to send telegrams and parcels to her in care of Reginald Faletti, and "his dedication to her never changed." Perhaps Alice was upset and angry because Bruno did not accompany her, perhaps she felt he was breaking their secret pact, or perhaps she was giving in to the mounting paranoia about Italy and Italians that was evident in her recent behavior. Whatever her reasons, she left instructions at Faletti's office to hold her mail and not to let anyone know where she was. Alice moved to Tucson, where she lived as a recluse, once again drinking heavily. One of her lawyers has suggested that she was unhappy, missing Bruno, wanting him to find her and apologize. All the while, Bruno continued to write and send telegrams; he mailed parcels and cards, but none ever reached Alice.

After several years of hearing nothing, fearful that Bruno may have fallen on hard times and concerned about his health, Alice asked her lawyers to try to locate him. Evidently they were unaware of the growing stack of mail at Faletti's office from the very man Alice sought. Through a law firm in Italy, the attorneys hired a private detective, who reported he was unable to locate Bruno, though it later turned out that no one had actually searched. When she heard he could not be found, Alice concluded Bruno had died, and she instructed her advisors to sell the Como villa.

Lawyer Arthur Gaudi with Price, Postel & Parma traveled to Milan to dispose of the house and make arrangements for the caretaker who had continued to live there; the man had established squatter's rights and built himself a home on the property. Gaudi remembers going from Milan to Como as though it were a scene from a movie—a terrifying drive on wet, winding roads through mountain passes. When he arrived, the villa appeared like a haunted house, utterly abandoned. In the center of the garden stood the hulking, burned relic of an enormous pine that had been struck by lightning. The tree seemed a fitting metaphor for the devastation of the couple's relationship. In their hasty departure, Alice and Bruno had simply left everything as it was—clothes, furniture, and personal items.

Towards the end of 1975, Alice established the trust commissioning Francis Price and Reginald Faletti, on her behalf, to purchase the El Mirasol Property from the Santa Barbara Museum of Art and to donate it to the city for a horticultural park. Even though she maintained her anonymity during the design and construction of the park, Alice remained involved from a distance. Landscape architect Grant Castleberg recalls providing sketches and later plans for approval by the donor. There were often delays of up to a month, he said, waiting for the donor's approval; he had no idea who she was, yet she never made suggestions or altered the plans. All communication was handled by the trustees and, most likely, Elizabeth de Forest. Clearly, however, Alice felt a sense of connection to the project: In her last telephone conversation with Willametta, Alice hoped that when her sister visited Santa Barbara, she "could go by my garden."

THE LEGAL CASE

After Alice's death in June 1977, newspaper headlines made public the bequest of her fortune to four local charities. Then six month later, Bruno's telegram—"Happy Santa Barbara's Day, thinking of you always"—arrived, addressed to Alice Leonarduzzi. Bruno's expression of love and affection for Alice complicated what had been a simple probate. It was clear that he was still alive, still considered himself married to Alice, and had no idea that she had died. Most important, it announced him as another potential heir. A fortune was at stake. Finding Bruno and settling the matter involved a multi-continent search over two years by at least six law firms and private investigators, and resulted in pages and pages of court documents.

Erythrina falcata
(Brazilian Coral Tree)

Santa Barbara Cemetery where Alice Keck Park was buried in 1977.

When Bruno was finally located in Italy after a lengthy search by another private detective, he ran away from Cooney, thinking the American was trying to kill him. Cooney chased Bruno down a slippery street in the rain and was able to serve legal notice only when the Italian fell on the wet pavement.

Bruno himself was not interested in Alice's money. But the legal events that had been put into motion could not be stopped. Price Postel and Parma, as executors, arranged separate legal counsel for Bruno by a prestigious law firm in Los Angeles. After many contested hearings and legal motions a negotiated settlement was agreed upon. Ironically, the delay had doubled the worth of Alice's estate. All her Superior Oil stock had soared in price, and the final value was close to fifty million dollars. Bruno received a five-million-dollar lump-sum payment, from which the Los Angeles law firm received more than two million dollars. Yet, as of 2004, Marino Bastianini believed Bruno had still not touched his fortune. And Michael Cooney confirmed that Bruno had never reached for any of the money Alice had deposited in his name in a Santa Barbara bank.

Under the law, an executor has a duty to find and notify anyone who might have a claim on an estate. Bruno's telegram suggested that he might be entitled to half—or possibly all—the fortune, a potentially monumental problem for the charities expecting to receive millions of dollars. Understandably, they questioned Bruno's standing.

Michael Cooney, at the time a young lawyer in Francis Price's law firm, recalls that he "spent parts of the next two years gumshoeing around Europe, Colorado and elsewhere exploring the meandering paths of two people he hadn't even met." He discovered, however, that Alice and Bruno, in addition to considering themselves married at the time of their secret pact, were also legally married under Colorado law: In 1970 they had purchased property in Rifle and held title in both names, Bruno and Alice Leonarduzzi.

Alice Keck Park's remains were interred in the Santa Barbara Cemetery on July 5, 1977. A simple headstone on a double plot marks her grave. It is a choice spot bordering the cliffs with a grand ocean view, overlooking the brilliant Pacific and across the channel to Santa Cruz and Anacapa Islands. Gulls and pelicans and cormorants glide on the wind currents. Below, on the rocky shore, more seabirds skitter on the sand. Dolphins and seals pass by, as do gray whales on their annual migration. For a woman who often rose at five in the morning to watch birds in the Colorado Rockies, it is a fitting resting place.

arellaga street

santa barbara street

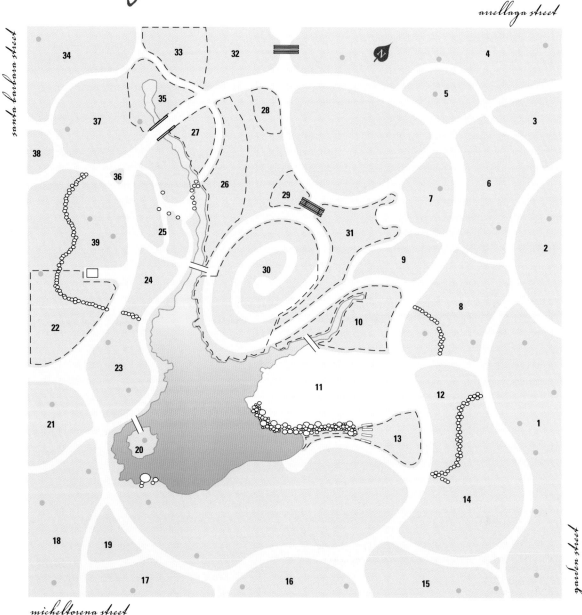

micheltorena street

garden street

Abelia floribunda (Mexican Abelia)
Evergreen, and almost ever blooming shrub. A graceful arching shrub with red-tinged leaves and reddish-purple flowers peaking in summer. *Caprifoliaceae* **22**

Abutilon hybridum (Chinese Lantern, Flowering Maple, Bellflower) Large, open-structured, evergreen shrub from South America with soft leaves, lobed like a maple, and blossoms year-round in a variety of colors. *Malvaceae* **25, 27**

Acacia podalyriifolia (Pearl Acacia)
A short-lived small tree or large shrub, from Australia, with light yellow, fluffy flowers, which are attractive against the silvery foliage, from November to February. *Fabaceae (Leguminosae)* **18**

Acanthus mollis (Bear's Breeches)
The Greeks and Romans copied the large leaf of this Mediterranean plant for the top of their most ornate columns. It has dark green, shiny decorative leaves up to 4 feet long and vertical flower stalks in late spring. *Acanthaceae* **31**

Acer palmatum (Japanese Maple)
A deciduous plant from Japan and Korea, with numerous named cultivars ranging from bonsai specimens to small trees. The foliage comes in many colors and may be simply palmate or so finely divided as to be thread-like. *Aceraceae* **1**

KEY

Botanic Name [Synonym] (Common Name) Plant description. *Family* **Location**

Achillea millefolium (Common Yarrow)
Plants from Europe and western Asia have white flowers, but pink-flowered plants can be seen on the Santa Barbara Channel Islands. Many named cultivars have been developed with flowers in shades of pink, lavender and red. This herbaceous perennial has long been used in the Mediterranean as a lawn. *Asteraceae (Compositae)* **39**

Aeonium hybrid (Aeonium) A succulent from the Canary Islands and Mediterranean with leaves arranged in precise geometric rosettes. Hybrids have been developed in different colors from 2 inches to 14 inches in diameter. *Crassulaceae* **6**

Aesculus × carnea 'Briotii' ('Briotii' Red Horsechestnut) A hybrid between Southeastern United States and Balkan horse chestnuts, it is a slow growing medium size tree which provides dense shade and red flowers in April-May. *Hippocastanaceae* **39**

Agapanthus orientalis hybrids (Lily-Of-The-Nile) This South African native is a popular perennial around the world. Evergreen clumps of linear leaves are attractive all year, and the large heads of blue or white flowers are very showy from April to August. *Amaryllidaceae* **2, 8**

Agave americana var. medio-picta 'Alba' (White Striped Century Plant) A small variegated version of the familiar big blue Century Plant from Mexico. It grows 3 to 4 feet tall, a bit wider, with white leaves margined with blue green. *Agavaceae* **6**

Agave attenuata (Foxtail Agave) A Mexican succulent with soft-tip blue-green rosettes, up to 3 feet in diameter, which forms colonies. They gradually become arborescent and then bloom with 8 to 12 foot stalks of pale yellow-green flowers. *Agavaceae* **25**

Agave parryi var. huachucensis Arizona and Mexico. Rounded rosettes of gray, spine-tipped leaves 18 to 24 inches in diameter form colonies. It eventually sends up a flower stalk, 18 to 20 feet, with yellow, brush-like flowers. *Agavaceae* **3**

Albizia julibrissin (Silk Tree) Fluffy pink flowers stand out on top of the fern-like foliage in summer on this graceful, small, spreading, deciduous tree from Australia. *Fabaceae (Leguminosae)* **10**

Aloe bainesii (Tree Aloe) Slow-growing yucca-like tree from South Africa, to 30 feet tall with heavy forking trunk and branches. Rosettes of 2-3 foot leaves and spikes of rose-pink flowers in winter. This is a very sculptural plant.
Asphodelaceae (Liliaceae) **3**

Aloe cilaris (Climbing Aloe) In the garden, it is climbing a palm tree near the pond island. Pencil-thick stems grow to 10 feet long with small, soft leaves and scarlet flower clusters year-round. South Africa *Asphodelaceae (Liliaceae)* **18**

Aloe plicatilis (Fan Aloe, Candelabra Aloe) A slow-growing arborescent shrub from South Africa with smooth grey-green 12 inch long leaves shaped like a menorah. Spikes of 18-inch scarlet flowers rise above the plant from August to October. *Asphodelaceae (Liliaceae)* **3**

Aloe species (Aloe) Several other Aloe species from South Africa can be found in the north corner of the Garden. *Asphodelaceae (Liliaceae)* **3, 4**

Aloe striata (Coral Aloe) Stemless, with small spines and blue green leaves. Coral flowers winter and spring on this attractive plant from stony hillsides in South Africa's Cape province. *Asphodelaceae (Liliaceae)* **4**

Alstroemeria psittacina (Peruvian Lily) Less showy than its highly hybridized siblings so valued by florists, this tuberous perennial from the Andes has delicate red and green flowers on 2 foot stems in late spring. *Liliaceae* **21**

Amaryllis belladonna [Brunsvigia rosea] (Naked Lady) Belladonna means beautiful lady, and this one has flowers on bare stems. Strap-like leaves rise from huge bulbs in November and disappear in spring to be followed by the fragrant, pink lily-like blossoms in August. *Amaryllidaceae* **8**

Anemone × hybrida [A. japonica] (Japanese Anemone, Windflower) A brief, but very showy flowering in the late summer - fall. Two to three foot stems rise above the low evergreen foliage with clusters of white or pink flowers, single or double. *Ranunculaceae* **34**

Anigozanthos hybrids (Kangaroo Paw) An unusual plant from Australia. Low, evergreen, sword-shaped leaves are topped by flower stalks ranging from 18 inches to 6 feet. The fuzzy flowers are pink, orange, red or chartreuse. *Haemodoraceae* **23, 30**

Aquilegia formosa (Western Columbine) A perennial native to western US. Bright red flowers on tall stems for a woodland garden. *Ranunculaceae* **25**

Arbutus 'Marina' (Strawberry Tree) A hybrid of uncertain parentage, but its similarity to *A. unedo*, from Ireland and Southern Europe, and the Madrone of the US west coast, is obvious. Hanging clusters of pink bell-shaped flowers appear year-round. The cinnamon-colored trunk and branches are like Madrone. *Ericaceae* **23**

Archontophoenix cunninghamiana [Seaforthia elegans] (King Palm) Australian import from the rainforests of New South Wales and Queensland. This elegant feather palm is used extensively as a landscape palm and street tree in Santa Barbara. *Arecaceae (Palmae)* **Santa Barbara Street**

Aristea ecklonii (Blue Stars) A member of the Iris family from Swaziland with evergreen grassy foliage and true-blue flowers in spring and summer. It re-seeds prolifically. *Iridaceae* **14**

Artemisia 'Powis Castle' (Silver Wormwood) Silvery, lacy foliage is the reason for growing this durable, 2 foot high by 4 to 6 foot wide shrub, but unfortunately, it is a short-lived plant.
Asteraceae (Compositae) **19**

Asparagus densiflorus 'Myers' (Myer's Asparagus) Green foxtails from South Africa. They contrast with Acanthus in the textural area northeast of the mound. *Liliaceae* **31**

Astelia chathamica 'Silver Spear' (Silver Spear) From the rain forests in New Zealand where it grows both on the ground and in trees. The soft silvery foliage contrasts well with other textures and colors along the dry creek at the south corner of the Garden. *Liliaceae* **18**

Azara microphylla (Boxleaf Azara) A graceful and delicate evergreen tree/shrub from the Chilean Andes. It grows 15-20 feet with a tan trunk and small shiny leaves. The inconspicuous yellow flowers are chocolate-scented in February and March. *Flacourtiaceae* **25**

Babiana stricta (Baboon Flower) So named because baboons reportedly dig and eat the corms. From South Africa and at home in southern California. It displays its jewel-tone red or blue blossoms in spring. *Iridaceae* **12**

Bauhinia forficata (Brazilian Orchid Tree) This semi-deciduous tree from Peru, Argentina and Brazil is taller and more upright than the other orchid trees in the park. It has deeply lobed leaves and narrow-petaled white flowers in fall. *Fabaceae (Leguminosae)* **14**

Bauhinia galpinii (Red Bauhinia) A semi-deciduous shrub from the South African tropics. It grows 6 to 8 feet tall and wide with a lovely, unusual shade of soft brick red flowers in summer. *Fabaceae (Leguminosae)* **30**

Bauhinia variegata (Purple Orchid Tree) Lavender or white flowers cover the bare branches in April and May, followed by many bean-like seedpods. This native of India and China is bare most of the year in our climate. *Fabaceae (Leguminosae)* **14, 1**

Bauhinia × blakeana (Hong Kong Orchid Tree) A natural hybrid between *B. variegata* and *B. purpurea*, It was discovered in Southern China in 1908 and later became the floral emblem of Hong Kong. Leaves and flowers are larger than either of its parents, and the flowers are of a more intense color. A small deciduous tree that blooms from fall through spring, and often during cool overcast days in summer.
Fabaceae (Leguminosae) **14**

Bergenia crassifolia (Winter Blooming Bergenia, Heart Leaved Bergenia) A perennial from China and the Himalayas which forms clumps of large, leathery, evergreen leaves. Pink clusters of small flowers on red stems from winter to early spring. *Saxifragaceae* **1**

Bidens ferulifolia A sprawling perennial from Southern US to Guatemala. It has bright yellow daisy flowers and is available in several named cultivars.
Asteraceae (Compositae) **9**

Bougainvillea cultivars (Bougainvillea) Bougainvillea comes from South America and is available in many named varieties with single and double flowers in white, pink, orange, purple and red. Most are vigorous vines which sprawl or climb by hooking long thorns on the host plant. Smaller varieties are available for use as groundcovers. *Nyctaginaceae* **16**

Bougainvillea spectabilis 'Rosenka' (Bougainvillea 'Rosenka') A cultivar which has become very popular since its introduction to Southern California. The flower color is pink in warm weather, coppery during the cool season. *Nyctaginaceae* **16**

Brahea armata (Mexican Blue Palm) This slow-growing fan palm from Baja California has pale silvery blue fronds, with a precise pattern, and large creamy-white inflorescences which radiate out from the fronds and droop gracefully. *Arecaceae (Palmae)* **15, 17**

Brugmansia hybrid [Datura hybrid] (Angel's Trumpet) A large shrub or small tree from the South American tropics with big, soft leaves and large trumpet flowers which hang gracefully during the warm months. White and a peach colored hybrids in the Sensory Garden are delightfully fragrant in the evening. *Solanaceae* **25, 39**

Butia capitata (Jelly Palm, Pindo Palm) A feather palm from Brazil, Uruguay and Argentina with recurving fronds of blue-gray. It is very slow growing, but can reach 20 feet in time. Spikes of creamy-white flowers are followed by yellow to red, edible fruit in summer *Arecaceae (Palmae)* **15, 17**

Calodendrum capense (Cape Chestnut) A lovely but temperamental flowering tree from South Africa. When conditions are to its liking, it develops into a shapely shade tree up to 40 feet tall and puts on a spectacular display of large clustered lavender flowers in June. *Rutaceae* **33**

Camellia japonica (Camellia) A long popular and much hybridized shrub from South-East Asia. It grows stiffly upright, eventually developing into a rounded tree 15 to 20 feet tall. The leaves are dark green and shiny, and buds, which form in summer open in winter to flowers up to 6 inches in diameter in a variety of forms. Blossoms are in shades of white, pink or red with many variegated forms. *Theaceae* **25**

Camellia sasanqua hybrids (Sasanqua Camellia) This evergreen Asian shrub is different from Camellia japonica in that the leaves and flowers are smaller and the plants have a looser form. There are many varieties and hybrids with other species. *Theaceae* **1**

Canna ×'Erebus,' Canna ×'Ra' (Water Canna Lily) Developed by Longwood Gardens in Pennsylvania for growing in water. 'Erebus' is salmon-pink and 'Ra' is yellow. From tropical America, it has been hybridized into many cultivars with large flower clusters in vibrant, warm colors. The 3 to 8 foot stems are clad with large leaves, and topped with flowers continuously from spring through fall. *Cannaceae* **10, 26**

Carissa macrocarpa hybrids (Natal Plum) This glossy shrub from Natal, South Africa has fragrant white pinwheel flowers followed by edible red fruit. Cultivars range from the 'Green Carpet' variety to the original species which grows to 8 feet tall. *Apocynaceae* **3, 4, 12, 13**

Cassia leptophylla (Gold Medallion Tree) Semi-evergreen 20 foot tree native to Brazil. Large bright yellow terminal clusters of flowers make a showy display in July and August , followed by long, brown seed pods. *Fabaceae (Leguminosae)* **18**

Ceiba insignis [Chorisia insignis] (White Flowering Floss Silk Tree) A spiny-trunked tree from South America to 20 feet tall. The white blossoms start in late fall on bare branches when its pink cousin is finished. The new foliage in spring is bright yellow, going through chartreuse to green when the fruit pops open to reveal silk balls. *Bombacaceae* **22, 39**

Ceiba speciosa [Chorisia speciosa] (Floss Silk Tree) Similar to *C. insignis*, but more upright in form. Several cultivars have been developed, including 'Los Angeles Beautiful' with wine-red flowers, and 'Majestic Beauty' with pink flowers on a more spreading tree and no thorns. Kapok comes from the seedpods. *Bombacaceae* **22**

Centaurea gymnocarpa (Dusty Miller) A woody perennial from Italy which grows 3 to 4 feet tall by 6 to 8 feet wide The soft, silvery twice-divided leaves are a good contrast with green. Purple thistle-like flowers appear in summer. *Asteraceae (Compositae)* **18, 21**

Centranthus ruber (Red Valerian) A Mediterranean native which spreads rapidly by stolons and seed in well-watered gardens The flowers are red, pink or white. *Valerianaceae* **23**

Cerastium tomentosum (Snow-In-Summer) Tiny white blossoms almost cover the mat of gray foliage in summer. A hardy groundcover from Europe. *Caryophyllaceae* **18, 21**

Cercis occidentalis (Western Redbud) A multi-trunk large shrub or small tree from the Sierra foothills of California. Small, magenta blossoms cling to the bare branches in early spring. Its graceful form and large, blue-green butterfly-shaped leaves are reason enough to grow this plant. *Fabaceae (Leguminosae)* **16**

Chamaedorea species One of many palms of this genus from Central and South America, most of which develop multiple stems and delicate fronds. The species in the Garden has fruit cluster with red stems and seeds. *Arecaceae (Palmae)* **26**

Chamaerops humilis (Mediterranean Fan Palm) The only palm tree native to Europe, occurring north and south of the Mediterranean Sea. Multiple trunks are covered with persistent hair-like fibers which are harvested commercially in Europe. The fronds stand out stiffly on this slow growing sculptural palm. *Arecaceae (Palmae)* **17**

Chasmanthe floribunda var. duckittii From South Africa, this deciduous member of the iris family has green sword-shaped leaves and spikes of canary yellow long-tubed flowers winter to early spring. The plant has naturalized in Southern California. The species has orange flowers. *Iridaceae* **39**

Chlorophytum comosum 'Variegatum' (Variegated Spider Plant) Usually seen as a hanging basket plant, this native of South Africa is a good groundcover for woodland areas. The small white blossoms are insignificant. *Liliaceae* **1**

Chondropetalum elephantinum (Large Cape Rush) A plant from the Restio family (South Africa) which grows 3 to 5 feet tall. The round dark green banded stems are topped with brown flowers. *Restionaceae* **21**

Cistus ×corbariensis [C. hybridus] (White Rock Rose) All the rockrose are from the Mediterranean. This white species grows 3 feet tall by 5 feet wide, and is an elegant, low maintenance plant for the drought tolerant garden. *Cistaceae* **21**

Cistus salvifolius (Sageleaf Rockrose) A low spreading shrub with small olive-green leaves and a profusion of small yellow-centered white flowers for a brief time in spring. *Cistaceae* **21**

Cistus 'Sunset' (Rockrose) A cultivar growing 2 feet tall by 6 feet wide with soft, gray leaves and bright magenta-pink flowers in spring and into summer. Flowering is less profuse than other rockrose, but for a longer time. *Cistaceae* **22**

Cistus 'Blanche' (White Rockrose) Perhaps the tallest rockrose, growing to 8 feet. The dark brownish-green foliage is topped by large pure white blossoms with yellow centers from spring into summer. *Cistaceae* **21**

Citrus sinensis 'Valencia' (Valencia Orange) These orange trees are remnants from El Mirasol Hotel where guests were free to harvest ripe fruit for a memorable taste of Santa Barbara. When the park was developed, Bruce Van Dyke, a local horticulturist, noticed the trees were rotted at the base of the trunks and would die unless this was corrected. The only way to preserve them was by a method called in-arching. Bruce, being experienced in this method, grafted a number of small orange twigs to bridge over the rotted area. In time, the grafts replaced the rotted part of the trunk so that today there is no evidence of the grafting and the trees are healthy and bearing fruit. *Rutaceae* **16**

Clematis lasiantha (Virgin's Bower) A deciduous vine native to California's chaparral which has volunteered in the Garden. Small white flowers appear in clusters in spring, followed by fluffy seed heads which blow in the wind. *Ranunculaceae* **6**

Clerodendrum bungei [C. foetidum] (Cashmere Bouquet) A perennial from China which grows rapidly from a mass of spreading roots, sending up 4 to 6 foot stems with large, coarse leaves that smell bad when bruised. During summer the stems are topped with 6 inch clusters of maroon buds which open to fragrant white flowers. *Verbenaceae* **25**

Clivia miniata 'Belgian Hybrid' (Kaffir Lily) From South Africa. The wild species has smaller, pale orange flowers and narrow, pointed leaves. Several hybrids were developed in northern Europe where *Clivia* is a popular house plant. Growers in the U.S. have recently taken an interest in the plant and have developed new hybrids in the yellow and salmon range. *Amaryllidaceae* **1, 6**

Clytostoma callistegioides [Bignonia violacea, B. speciosa] (Violet Trumpet Vine) A vigorous vine from Brazil with 2-part glossy, green leaves and violet, cinnamon-scented flowers, spring to fall. It readily climbs anything and is a natural for chain-link fences. *Bignoniaceae* **38**

Cocculus laurifolius (Himalayan Laurel) An evergreen shrub or small multi-stem tree 20-25 feet and wider. This Himalayan native is grown for its elegant leaves which have 3 prominent parallel veins. *Menispermaceae* **6**

Coleonema album [Diosma alba] (White Breath-Of-Heaven) A plant from South Africa with scented foliage and a low mounded form. It has white flowers set against the dark green fine-textured foliage. *Rutaceae* **28**

Convolvulus sabatius [C. mauritanicus] (Ground Morning Glory) A small, spreading herbaceous plant from the Mediterranean with azure-blue flowers from spring through fall. *Convulvulaceae* **23**

Correa 'Dusky Bells' (Australian Fuchsia) The Correas are versatile, drought-tolerant plants from Australia, and this one is an elegant groundcover for any exposure. The foliage is an unusual green and the flowers are dusty-pink. *Rutaceae* **1**

Correa 'Ivory Bells' (Australian Fuchsia) Ivory Bells has white flowers on a gray shrub which slowly grows to 4 feet by 4 feet. *Rutaceae* **24**

Corymbia ficifolia [Eucalyptus ficifolia] (Red Flowering Gum) Often used as a street tree where its base grows over the curb and sidewalk. It is not a graceful eucalyptus, but it makes up for that with its brilliant clusters of cream, light pink, salmon, orange or red flowers peaking in July and August. *Myrtaceae* **2, 6**

Cotoneaster buxifolius (Boxwood Cotoneaster) A gray shrub from China with tiny leaves which are covered with fine gray hairs. It grows 3 to 5 feet tall, spreading wider. It has small white flowers in spring and red berries in fall for a fire and smoke effect. *Rosaceae* **8, 12**

Cotoneaster dammeri (Bearberry Cotoneaster) A low-growing shrub from China, used as a groundcover and often sheared to 6 inches tall. It has small, shiny green leaves, little white flowers in spring and a profusion of red berries in fall. There are several cultivars. *Rosaceae* **6**

Cotoneaster salicifolia 'Herbstfeuer' (Willow-Leaf Cotoneaster) One of several cultivars of a tall evergreen species from China. This variety is a low spreading shrub 2 to 3 feet tall and 8 to 10 feet wide. *Rosaceae* **1**

Crassula multicava (Fairy Crassula) A delicate plant which is a member of a large South African family. It is a good groundcover in sun or shade. In spring the plants are covered with delicate dusty-pink flowers. When the blooms fade, small plantlets appear along the stems developing into new plants if they touch moist ground. Due to its shallow roots, it grows well under greedy trees such as Eucalyptus. *Crassulaceae* **4**

Crinum × powellii 'Album' (Crinum Lily) Many Crinums have deciduous foliage and bloom on naked stems, like Amaryllis, but this hybrid is evergreen with long, wavy-edged bright green foliage. The large, fragrant flowers resemble Easter lilies and bloom in great profusion from spring into summer. *Liliaceae* **32**

Cuphea ignea (Cigar Plant) This native of Mexico and Central America has orange-red tubular flowers attractive to hummingbirds. It blooms throughout the warm months on a sprawling, viny shrub. *Lythraceae* **30**

Cuphea micropetala Similar to *Cuphea ignea*, but a more substantial plant with larger leaves and flowers and a tendency to bloom year-round. *Lythraceae* **30**

Cyperus albostriatus (Broad-leaf umbrella plant) A diminutive reed from South Africa. It has 2 foot stems with a whorl of leaves topped by delicate flowers. *Cyperaceae* **26**

Cyperus papyrus (Papyrus) Our word "paper" comes from this African bog plant, because the triangular stems were used by the Egyptians to make scrolls. The 6 to 8 foot reeds are topped by graceful clusters of green filaments. *Cyperaceae* **26**

Dahlia imperialis (Tree Dahlia) A woody perennial which sends up 12 foot stalks each year from a perennial root system. A cluster of lavender cosmos-like flowers in late fall top each stem. The 'Alba' variety has white flowers. *Asteraceae (Compositae)* **22**

Davallia trichomanoides (Squirrel's Foot Fern) An epiphytic fern from Malaysia and Indonesia that is usually grown in hanging baskets. The plants in the park are growing in the ground. *Polypodiaceae* **1**

Dianella tasmanica (Flax Lily) From Australia and Tasmania, this stoloniferous (spreads by roots), sword-leaf plant is a natural groundcover under trees. The white flowers have an airy appeal, but the real attraction is the iridescent violet berries in summer. 'Variegata' has attractive white-striped foliage. *Liliaceae* **29, 31**

Dietes vegeta [Moraea iridioides] (Fortnight Lily) Aptly-named because it blooms at the full and new moons from spring through fall. An attractive sword-leaf perennial which forms a large clump. The flowers are white and violet with an orange dot. Since the flower stems are perennial, lasting many years, they should not be removed after each flowering. However, it is a good idea to remove the individual seed pods to prevent re-seeding. *Iridaceae* **7**

Dombeya cacuminum (Strawberry Snowball Tree) A large, fast growing evergreen column to 50 feet tall with dark green maple-like leaves. Magnificent coral flower clusters hang under the foliage in January and February spreading a colorful carpet under the tree. *Sterculaceae* **12**

Dombeya calantha This *Dombeya* is a small tree or large shrub with small clusters of pale lavender-pink flowers in the typical pendant fashion. *Sterculaceae* **12**

Doryanthes palmerii (Spear Lilly) The largest showy member of the lily family with 6 foot sword-shaped leaves and curious 6 to 8 foot spikes of red-orange flowers for several months in spring and early summer. Hummingbirds are attracted to the sticky flowers of this Australian native. *Liliaceae* **6**

Duchesnea indica (Indian Mock Strawberry) A low-growing strawberry relative from Japan and southern Asia which tends to appear here and there in gardens. Yellow flowers are followed by red fruit which looks like alpine strawberries, but is insipid. *Rosaceae* **18**

Duranta erecta [D. repens] (Pigeon Berry, Sky Flower) A sprawling tender evergreen shrub or small tree from South Florida to Brazil. It forms a multi-stemmed clump up to 18 feet tall and wide with pendulous branches. The light blue flowers appear off and on throughout the year, as does the orange fruit. *Verbenaceae* **7**

Dypsis decaryi [Neodypsis decaryi] (Triangle Palm) The trunk is triangular in cross section with sets of 3 equally spaced gray-green fronds. A drought-tolerant, slow-growing feather palm from the dry side of Madagascar. Ultimate height is 15 to 20 feet. *Arecaceae (Palmae)* **17**

Echium fastuosum (Pride Of Madeira) Rapid growing and woody, this perennial has towers of nectar rich flowers ranging from turquoise blue through pure blue to purple. Because of its large size and short life (4 to 8 years) it is best suited to hillsides where its drought-tolerance and habit of re-seeding can be an advantage. *Boraginaceae* **21**

Eichhornia crassipes (Water Hyacinth)
This lovely floating aquatic plant has azure-blue flowers throughout the warm season. It multiplies rapidly in nutrient-rich water and has become a serious pest in semi-tropical waterways. Because it grows only in "dirty" water, it has great possibilities for removing pollutants, including heavy metals, from water. *Pontederiaceae* **10**

Elegia capensis (Horsetail Restio)
One of several Restios from South Africa. Their natural habitat is along water-courses. The 6 foot plant has delicate thread-like foliage on arching stems like *Equisetum*. *Restionaceae* **26**

Erythrina caffra (African Coral Tree)
A large, spreading tree from South Africa which is equally at home in Southern California where it grows rapidly. It loses its leaves in December and blossoms begin to unfold in January continuing into spring. *Fabaceae (Leguminosae)* **31**

Erythrina crista-galli (Cockspur Coral Tree) A small, thorny, deciduous tree which bears loose clusters of red flowers sporadically from spring through fall. *Fabaceae (Leguminosae)* **31**

Erythrina falcata (Brazilian Coral Tree)
A nearly-evergreen, upright coral tree to 40 feet tall with a 30 foot spread and an extensive surface root system. Another rapid grower, it has hanging clusters of bright red flowers in May and June. *Fabaceae (Leguminosae)* **30**

Erythrina humeana (Natal Coral Tree)
A small tree from South Africa with orange-red flowers from August through November. The blossoms attract hummingbirds. *Fabaceae (Leguminosae)* **9**

Erythrina × bidwillii This large deciduous shrub or small tree grows to 20 feet. It has an excellent display of two foot long clusters of ruby-red flowers on willowy stalks from spring into late fall. It is very thorny and inclined towards an unattractive form unless it is carefully pruned. *Fabaceae (Leguminosae)* **9**

Erythrina × sykesii (Australian Coral Tree) A hybrid coral tree from Australia, it grows 20-30 feet tall and a bit wider, with a tan trunk. Showy red flowers appear from January to March before the leafy canopy fills in. It is more manageable than *E. caffra* due to its smaller size and sturdier branches. *Fabaceae (Leguminosae)* **31**

Escallonia 'Newport Dwarf' The parents are from South America, mostly Chile. This is a smaller cultivar with tiny, glossy, dark green leaves and red flowers on a 4 to 5 foot dense shrub. Very attractive when young, it gets brushy in old age. *Escalloniaceae* **26**

Eucomis bicolor (Pineapple Lily)
Deciduous perennials from South Africa which grow from tuberous roots. This species bears pineapple-like spikes of green-white flowers during the summer. Numerous hybrids are available with flowers in pink, yellow and red. *Liliaceae* **32**

Euphorbia characias ssp. wulfenii
A succulent shrub from the Mediterranean, growing 3 to 6 feet tall and wider, with gray-green foliage and large clusters of chartreuse flowers in spring and summer. *Euphorbiaceae* **18**

Euphorbia species The single specimen in the Garden is a South African species with the characteristic branching, columnar form. *Euphorbiaceae* **4**

Fatsia japonica [Aralia seiboldii, A. japonica] (Japanese Aralia) A tropical-appearing shrub from Korea and Japan which is an old standby for shady areas. The large, durable, dark green palmate leaves grow on leafless stems to 10 feet. White flowers in winter are followed by black fruit. *Araliaceae* **26**

Festuca elatior ssp. arundinacea hybrid (Lawn, Meadow Fescue) What started as a coarse pasture grass in Europe and Asia has been refined into the most popular lawn grass for Southern California, replacing bluegrass which was never at home here. *Poaceae* **Lawn**

Festuca ovina var. glauca (Blue Fescue) A temperate grass from Europe which will grow in most climates. It makes an attractive, small clump with delicate white flower stalks in summer. The cultivar 'Elija Blue' emphasizes the blue color. *Poaceae* **18, 21**

Festuca rubra (Creeping Red Fescue)
From Europe and North America, it grows in most climates from the Arctic to the lower sub-tropical climates. A lawn grass in temperate climates, it dies-out if mown in Southern California and is grown here as an unmown slope cover. The native California subspecies 'Mutatta' has a bluish tinge and is moderately drought-tolerant. *Poaceae* **30**

Ficus auriculata [F. roxburghii] (Roxburgh's Fig) A small semi-deciduous tree from India which can reach a height and spread of 25 feet. It has large sand-papery leaves and an abundance of fruit on the trunk and branches, which suggest its best use is away from paving. *Moraceae* **39**

Ficus benghalensis (Banyan) A tender tropical fig tree from India and Pakistan which grows slowly in our climate, and is not very large. It has thick leaves and red fruit in abundance. In warm humid climates, the branches send aerial roots to the ground and the tree grows laterally, indefinitely. *Moraceae* **32**

Ficus benjamina (Weeping Chinese Banyan) A beautiful evergreen tree, from the wetter parts of India, which is a popular houseplant. It is grown extensively in frost-free areas of Southern California, and is often planted next to a house, which can be a problem as the roots grow into the foundation. In time it becomes a large tree. *Moraceae* **39**

Ficus carica (Edible Fig) The tree in the park is likely a bird-planted seedling, as the fruit is barely edible. Fig trees are mentioned many times in the Bible, as this eastern Mediterranean fruit has been grown for several thousand years. *Moraceae* **39**

Francoa ramosa (Maiden's Weath)
From Chile, a perennial for the shade garden with low basal foliage and graceful stems of white or lavender flowers in summer. *Saxifragaceae* **25**

Freesia refracta (Freesia) This little jewell from South Africa is well adapted to our climate. The florist industry has developed many varieties in brilliant colors with long stems, which have retained some of the fragrance, but cannot rival that of the species which is low growing with small white, yellow and pale lavender flowers. *Iridaceae* **22, 23**

Gaura lindheimeri A prairie plant from the American southwest. It is a delicate, deciduous perennial growing 2 to 3 feet tall with many stalks of white to pink flowers. There are several cultivars with more colorful flowers and variegated foliage. *Onagraceae* **32**

Gazania hybrids (African Daisy, Gazania) From South Africa. Several Gazania species have been hybridized and developed into varieties in all the warm colors and shades of burgundy and lavender. It is a tough, low perennial groundcover with an abundance of blossoms through-out the year on the coast, peaking in early spring. *Asteraceae (Compositae)* **8, 14**

Gelsemium sempervirens (Carolina Jessamine) A delicate vine growing 10 to 15 feet by twining, it has light green leaves with a bamboo-like quality. Vivid yellow flowers add a cheerful note to the Garden in winter. *Loganiaceae* **25**

Geranium maderense This bold native of Madeira is quite different from most geraniums; the plant, leaves and flowers are much larger and the flower color is more intense. It is a biennial, which means it takes two years or more to develop blossoms—a woodland plant left to re-seed for flowers every year. *Geraniaceae* **22**

Geranium × cantabrigiense 'Biokovo' (Cranesbill) A hybrid of two species and the most prevalent cranesbill in Southern California gardens, due largely to its adaptability. It is an attractive groundcover at the edge of a border or under open shrubs. *Geraniaceae* **25**

Ginkgo biloba 'Autumn Gold' (Chinese Maidenhair Tree) Leaf fossils 200,000,000 years-old have been found of this tree around the world, but it now occurs in only 2 locations in China. This deciduous tree is actually related to conifers but with fan-shaped leaves which develop a bright yellow fall color, even in our mild climate. *Ginkgoaceae* **36**

Gleditsia triacanthos var. inermis 'Shademaster' (Honey Locust) The original species comes from Pennsylvania, Nebraska and Texas where it may have huge thorns and a long deciduous season. This cultivar with light-textured compound leaves is a small, thornless tree. *Fabaceae (Leguminosae)* **31**

Hedychium gardnerianum (Kahili Ginger) One of many tuberous cane-like perennials in this genus, each with a distinctive fragrance. This native of India bears foot tall blossoms of red and yellow in August with a strong, spicy fragrance. The plant grows 3 to 5 feet tall. *Zingiberaceae* **1, 26**

Helianthus tuberosa (Jerusalem Artichoke, Iroquois Potato) The tuberous roots of this native American were used by Indians as food and medicine. The sunflower blossoms appear on top of 5 to 8 foot stems in the summer and fall. *Asteraceae (Compositae)* **4**

Helichrysum petiolare 'Limelight' (Licorice Plant) From South Africa. This cultivar of a large, fast growing woody perennial is much more restrained, even fragile . With ideal conditions, its chartreuse foliage is a refreshing contrast to dark green or purple. *Asteraceae (Compositae)* **27**

Helictotrichon sempervirens (Blue Oat Grass) A grass from the western Mediterranean, similar to blue fescue, but larger, making an 18 to 24 inch clump. White flowers in summer add a delicate texture. Drought-tolerant and evergreen. *Poaceae* **36**

Heliotropium arborescens (Heliotrope) A large sprawling shrub From Peru which has light green leaves and year-round fragrant lavender flowers. It is better known through several hybrids which are much smaller and have dark, attractively ribbed foliage, dark purple flowers and the same cherry pie fragrance. *Boraginaceae* **18, 21**

Hemerocallis hybrids (Daylily) A popular garden plant for centuries, it has been hybridized into many named cultivars in all colors except true blue. The newer hybrids have flowers lasting several days. The orange variety next to the pond is evergreen. *Liliaceae* **18**

Hibbertia scandens [H.volubilis] (Guinea Gold Vine) A tidy, small vine from Australia, with yellow poppy-like flowers blooming through spring and summer. It is handsome growing up, or trailing over a wall. *Dilleniaceae* **30**

Hibiscus rosa-sinensis (Hibiscus) A signature plant of the tropics and the official flower of Santa Barbara. The large flowers of this Southeast Asian plant are single or double in all the warm colors and pure white. Subject to the giant Mexican whitefly. *Malvaceae* **12**

Homeria collina (Cape Tulip) One of many South African plants in the iris family growing in the park, this one has thin grassy foliage with delicate flowers in the warm pastel shades - spring. *Iridaceae* **23**

Hyacinthoides hispanica [Scilla hispanica, Scilla campanulata] (Spanish Bluebell) As the name implies, it looks like hyacinth and is native to the Iberian Peninsula. It grows to eighteen inches tall with flowers of white, pink or blue in late winter. *Liliaceae* **6**

Hymenosporum flavum (Sweetshade) An Australian native which, like its *Pittosporum* cousins, emits a delicious fragrance from its tubular yellow flowers - March and April. A slender, evergreen tree from 20-40 feet tall. *Pittosporaceae* **9,10**

Hypericum 'Rowallane' (St. Johnswort) This hybrid, from County Down in Ireland, is an open, brushy, evergreen shrub to 6 feet tall. The yellow flowers are 3 inches across and appear in summer and fall. *Hypericaceae* **30**

Ilex cornuta 'Berries Jubilee' (Holly) One of many cultivars of the Chinese holly, it grows to 4 to 5 feet tall and wider. The leaves are larger and spinier than most of the other cultivars. It has an abundant crop of bright red berries through fall and winter. *Aquifoliaceae* **31**

Ipheion uniflorum [Brodiaea uniflora, Triteleia uniflora] (Starflower) This cheerful little bulb from Argentina has low grassy foliage in winter which is covered in small, pale blue flowers in spring. The cultivars have larger flowers ranging from white to a medium blue. The plants colonize and make a lovely seasonal groundcover in a woodland garden. *Liliaceae* **8**

Iris germanica hybrid (German Iris, Bearded Iris) Iris is the Greek Goddess of the Rainbow and her namesake plants come in all those colors, plus white and a near black. The blue-green sword-like foliage adds a vertical element to the Garden even after the spring blooms are finished. Some varieties are re-blooming, with flowers on and off all year. *Iridaceae* **35**

Iris orientalis [I. ochroleuca] (Yellow Band Iris) Essentially a bog plant, it has a short but lovely blooming season with tall stems of white flowers. Tolerates considerable drought and is a handsome vertical accent for the perennial border, or at the edge of a pond. *Iridaceae* **34, 37**

Iris pseudacorus (Yellow Flag Iris) Similar to *I. orientalis*, but with yellow flowers. Cultivars offer variegated foliage and softer flower colors. *Iridaceae* **34, 37**

Iris 'Nada' (Butterfly Iris) One of a group of semi-tropical crested iris. It has graceful, evergreen sword-shaped leaves and, in the spring, a profusion of branched stems of small white, orchid-like flowers. *Iridaceae* **35**

Iris 'Pacific Coast Hybrids' (Pacific Coast Iris) These lovely hybrids, of up to seven species native to the west coast, form evergreen clumps of horizontal grassy foliage 12 inches tall and 3 feet or more across. The flowers come in many named cultivars in all the iris colors, some with the attractive veining of their *I. innominata* parentage. *Iridaceae* **27, 35**

Ixia maculata (African Corn Lily) Grassy foliage emerges from corms with the first winter rain. This is followed by 20 inch stems bearing tubular flowers in warm pastel colors. *Iridaceae* **22, 23**

Jacaranda mimosifolia (Jacaranda) This native of Brazil is Santa Barbara's most prevalent street tree with a shapely form to 40 feet tall by 30 feet wide. There is a spectacular display of azure-blue flowers from late April through June followed by fern-like foliage. A lesser flowering occurs in August. *Bignoniaceae* **2**

Jasminum le-ratii (Privet-Leaved Jasmine) A vine/shrub from New Caledonia. It is usually seen as a formless shrub, but takes well to the shears for use in formal gardens. Its small star-shaped white flowers appear in spring and have a delicate scent. *Oleaceae* **39**

Kniphofia hybrid (Red Hot Poker, Torch Lily) Clumps of grass-like foliage may be evergreen or deciduous, depending on the parentage. The stalks of tubular flowers come in all the warm shades and appear from spring through fall—except for the variety 'Christmas Cheer'. *Liliaceae* **36**

Koelreuteria bipinnata (Chinese LanternTree) A beautiful tree in all aspects, it develops slowly, forming a symmetrical canopy for the perfect shade tree. The leaves are attractively divided, and the yellow flowers in late summer last only a week, but the crowning glory is the salmon-colored seed capsules which come immediately from the flowers and hold until the foliage falls in early winter. *Sapindaceae* **13**

Lantana hybrids (Lantana) Plants range from low groundcovers to tall shrubs and the year-round flowers come in many shades of red, pink, yellow, lavender and white. *Lantana camara*, from tropical America, spreads rapidly and has been declared a pest in Hawaii. *Verbenaceae* **30**

Lantana montevidensis [L. sellowiana] (Trailing Lantana) A rapidly spreading herbaceous plant, from tropical South America, growing 12 to 30 inches in height. The tenacious root system makes it a useful soil binder on steep slopes. New varieties have been developed with pure white and variegated lavender and white blossoms. *Verbenaceae* **14**

Laurus nobilis (Sweet Bay, Grecian Laurel) The Laurel of the ancients, sacred to Apollo and commonly planted in temple gardens. It is a columnar, evergreen tree to 40 feet tall. Bay leaves are used for flavoring foods. *Lauraceae* **15**

Lavandula angustifolia (English Lavender) The species is native to the mountains of Southern Europe and quickly grows to 4 feet tall and 6 feet wide with slender, year-round spikes of purple flowers. The common name refers to the many dwarf cultivars which were developed in England, and seem to prefer that climate. *Lamiaceae (Labiatae)* **22**

Lavandula dentata var. candicans (French Lavender) A sprawling shrub to 2 feet tall and 6 feet wide with gray foliage and lavender blossoms all year. The species has light green leaves and is less vigorous. *Lamiaceae (Labiatae)* **23**

Lavandula 'Goodwin Creek' (Lavender) A neat, rounded, hybrid shrub growing 2 to 3 feet tall and a bit wider. It has dark violet flowers year-round in our mild coastal climate. *Lamiaceae (Labiatae)* **23**

Leonotis leonurus (Lion's Tail) A very showy member of the mint family from South Africa. It grows 4 to 6 feet tall with whorls of orange flowers on vertical stems - spring to fall. *Lamiaceae (Labiatae)* **30**

Leptospermum laevigatum (Australian Tea Tree) Tea tree because Captain Cook brewed a beverage from the leaves for his sailors to prevent scurvy. The specimen in the Garden, at the east corner, is a natural work of art with its heavy, wandering, twisted branches. It takes time to achieve this sculptural effect. A pliable plant, often trimmed as a hedge or trained on a pergola for shade. *Myrtaceae* **1**

Leptospermum laevigatum 'Reevesii' (Australian Tea Bush) A compact version of the species which grows 4 feet tall and a bit wider. The interest is in the dense undulating form and the refined texture of the blue-gray foliage color. *Myrtaceae* **21**

Leucaena esculenta (Guaje) A deciduous tree from southern Texas and Mexico with fern-like compound leaves; clusters of white pompon like flowers appear in fall and winter. The leaves and branch structure are the main attractions. *Fabaceae (Leguminosae)* **11**

Leucojum aestivum (Summer Snowflake) A native of Europe with a misleading common name, because the plant blooms in winter. The foliage is dark green and strap-like and the white, nodding bell flowers have a green dot on each petal. *Amaryllidaceae* **14**

Leymus condensatus 'Canyon Prince' (Blue Giant Wild Rye) Found growing on Prince Island in Cuyler's Harbor at San Miguel Island and given Santa Barbara Botanic Garden's signature "Canyon" name. This silvery blue grass grows 3 to 4 feet tall and slowly spreads by rhizomes. The spikes of white flowers grow above the foliage. *Poaceae* **18**

Libertia grandiflora (New Zealand Iris) A 2 foot plant with green sword-shaped leaves and clusters of white flowers on stems above the foliage late spring to mid-summer. *Iridaceae* **32**

Limonium perezii (Sea Lavender, Statice) A perennial from the Canary Islands which grows 2 to 3 feet tall and as wide. It has wavy, dark green basal leaves and year-round purple bracts and white flowers The papery quality of the bracts makes it a natural for dried bouquets. *Plumbaginaceae* **22**

Liquidambar styraciflua (American Sweetgum) The name refers to the fragrant balsamic resin, styrax, obtained from the American and Asiatic species. it is used in perfumes, soaps, incense, lacquers, medicines, and as a flavoring for tobacco. Palmate, five to seven lobed leaves and fall foliage color mistakenly suggest that this is a maple. *Hamamelidaceae* **11**

Liriope muscari (Lilyturf) The green species of this evergreen Asian grass-like plant, from which many hybrids have been developed, grows 18 inches tall and has spikes of purple flowers in summer. *Liliaceae* **36**

Liriope muscari 'Silvery Sunproof' (Lilyturf) The creamy white and green striped leaves give this perennial a fresh look. The lilac blossoms are a bonus to the soft foliage. It really does not like full sun. *Liliaceae* **27**

Liriope spicata 'Silver Dragon' (Variegated Lilyturf) A rapid spreader, even growing into masonry cracks. It differs from 'Silvery Sunproof' in the variegation colors, which have an overall gray effect, and in the stiffer leaves. The pale lavender flowers are insignificant. *Liliaceae* **25**

Lonicera confusa (Honeysuckle) A more compact plant than the common Japanese honeysuckle, it can easily be kept as a small, trailing shrub. It has blue-green leaves and white to yellow flowers with a delicious fragrance. *Caprifoliaceae* **25**

Lophostemon confertus [Tristania conferta] (Brisbane Box) A medium-size broad leaf evergreen tree here, but much larger in Australia. It has tan, mottled, exfoliating bark and puffy myrtle blossoms. *Myrtaceae* **Arrellaga Street**

Loropetalum chinense hybrid (Fringe Flower) There are several of the many hybrids in the Garden. The colors can range from a spring touch of bronze, fading to green, to a rather dark purple all season. The bright pink flowers, appear intermittently throughout the year. They are fast growing shrubs ranging from 3 feet to 12 feet in height and spreading wider with an attractive arching form. China and Japan. *Hamamelidaceae* **25, 26, 30**

Luma apiculata [Myrtus luma] From Chile and Argentina. A shrub 6 to 8 feet tall with small, thick dark green leaves and small single flowers in the fall, followed by black fruit. An alternative to myrtle or boxwood. *Myrtaceae* **38**

Lycianthes rantonnetii [Solanum rantonnetii] (Paraguay Nightshade) Indigo-blue flowers with a yellow center will, at times, totally cover this very rapid-growing large, sprawling, semi-deciduous shrub. Newer varieties, such as 'Royal Robe' are evergreen and more compact. *Solanaceae* **32**

Magnolia grandiflora (Southern Magnolia, Bull Bay Tree) A massive tree to 125 feet, in its native Southeast US, but smaller here. Evergreen, large, dark glossy oval shaped leaves are rusty beneath. Large, white, fragrant flowers appear from spring through fall. *Magnoliaceae* **4, 28, 29**

Magnolia × soulangeana (Saucer Magnolia) This deciduous hybrid grows as a large multi-trunk shrub or small tree with leaves that are lighter green and thinner than *Magnolia grandiflora*. There are many varieties ranging from white through pink to purple. In mild winter climates the large blossoms appear at Christmas on bare branches. *Magnoliaceae* **22**

Malvaviscus arboreus (Turk's Cap) Large, thin, velvety, light green leaves cover this sprawling shrub to 12 feet tall which can spread indefinitely by underground runners (stolons). Small, red bell-shaped flowers appear sparsely year-round and are followed by an interesting white fruit. *Malvaceae* **30**

Markhamia lutea [M. hildebrandtii] (Markhamia) A medium-sized broadleaf evergreen tree from tropical Africa. It grows 25-35 feet tall with rough, dark green leaves and bright yellow clusters of 2 inch trumpet-shaped flowers in summer, which are followed by slender bean pods. *Bignoniaceae* **34**

Maytenus boaria (Mayten Tree) An evergreen tree from the wetter areas of Chile. It has tiny, light green leaves on long, graceful branchlets similar to weeping willow. Slow to moderate growth rate eventually 30 feet tall with 15-20 foot spread, but usually smaller. The cultivar 'Green Showers' has darker, denser foliage and a more symmetrical form. *Celastraceae* **38**

Melianthus major (Honeybush) South Africa. A large sprawling shrub, 8 to 10 feet tall and wide with blue-green compound leaves. The nectar rich mahogany colored flower stalks rise above the foliage in late winter and are a major attraction to hummingbirds and song birds. *Melianthaceae* **18**

Metrosideros excelsa (New Zealand Christmas Tree) A medium size rounded or spreading tree from New Zealand where it covers coastal hills. The dark red flowers bloom in December in New Zealand, June and July here. The foliage is dense, dark green on top and wooly-white beneath. In humid climates, red aerial roots drop from the trunk and branches. *Myrtaceae* **18**

Michelia figo [M. fuscata] (Banana Shrub) A slow-growing, evergreen shrub from China. It reaches 10 to 12 feet tall and 6 to 8 feet wide with glossy medium green leaves. The yellow flowers appear from March to May with a fragrance reminiscent of ripe bananas. *Magnoliaceae* **30**

Miscanthus sinensis condensatus 'Cosmopolitan' (Cosmopolitan Silver Grass) A tall semi-evergreen grass from East Asia with wide leaf blades striped green and white. Copper-colored blossoms appear in summer and fade to white in fall. *Poaceae* **27**

Miscanthus sinensis (Maiden Grass) From Japan, Korea and China, this is a tall grass—3 to 7 feet, depending on the variety. The green species has stalks of copper-red flowers in the fall that grow above the foliage. *Poaceae* **18**

Miscanthus sinensis 'Morning Light' (Variegated Maiden Grass) A variegated cultivar of the above. *Poaceae* **18**

Montanoa grandiflora (Mexican Daisy Tree) A shrub to 12 feet tall with large deeply cut leaves. Three inch daisy-like flowers in fall and winter smell like freshly-baked cookies. Brown seed heads can be used in dried arrangements. *Asteraceae (Compositae)* **4**

Murraya paniculata [M. exotica] (Orange Jessamine) A large evergreen shrub from Southeast Asia, growing 6 to 15 feet tall and wide. It has dark green glossy leaves which are divided into 5 to 9 leaflets. The white flowers with a jasmine fragrance appear in late summer and fall, followed by small red fruit. A compact form is sold as *Murraya exotica. Rutaceae* **37**

Myrtus communis (Myrtle) A small tree from the Mediterranean which is usually seen in the variety 'Compacta' as a sheared hedge. White, fragrant flowers sparkle against the dark green leaves in summer and are followed by black berries. The leaves have been used for centuries to add a scent to soap. *Myrtaceae* **20**

Narcissus hybrid (Narcissus) Several varieties of this bulb are growing in the Garden, including the paper whites with licorice scented flowers in the fall, tiny jonquil varieties and the old favorite, daffodil. The many species come from areas around the Mediterranean. *Amaryllidaceae* **14**

Nepeta × faassenii (Catmint) A hybrid between 2 species from southern Europe and the Mideast. It grows 1 foot tall and spreads wider, with soft, small gray-green leaves and spikes of violet-blue flowers in spring and summer. *Lamiaceae (Labiatae)* **23**

Nerium oleander (Oleander) Street trees on Micheltorena are an old double pink variety. The sweet-scented blossoms cover the plants during the warm months. It has a reputation as a poisonous plant, but there is no documentation of human deaths attributable to this shrub. *Apocynaceae* **Micheltorena Street**

Nymphaea hybrid (Waterlily) From a few plants in pots in 1979, the foliage now covers much of the pond. This is one of the longer blooming creamy-white varieties, starting in spring and continuing until Christmas. *Nymphaea* **Pond**

Olea europaea (Mission Olive) Introduced to California by Franciscan missionaries for the oil from its black fruit, this medium size, evergreen tree with gray-green leaves is a popular landscape specimen. Old trees develop beautiful trunk and root patterns. There are trees several thousand years old in its Mediterranean homeland. *Oleaceae* **23**

Ophiopogon jaburan [Liriope gigantea] (Giant Lily Turf) From Asia. This large lily turf forms a grassy clump to 3 feet tall and wide. Violet-blue flowers appear in summer. *Liliaceae* **18, 22**

Oxalis purpurea 'Grand Duchess' (Oxalis) From The Cape of Good Hope in South Africa. Small plant with large, clover-like leaves and funnel shaped flowers of pink, white or lavender from fall into spring. All Oxalis can be invasive; Grand Duchess has spread throughout the park. *Oxalidaceae* **15, 23**

Pachypodium lamerei (Madagascar Palm) An odd plant which sends up a very thorny, branching trunk to 18 feet tall. It looks like a Plumeria with thorns, including the fragrant, white flowers. *Apocynaceae* **4**

Parkinsonia aculeata (Jerusalem Thorn, Mexican Palo Verde) Rapid growth when young, then slowing to produce a light, airy-looking desert plant with yellow green bark and spiny branches. A native of southwestern US and Mexico, 15-20 feet tall and wide. Prolific yellow flowers in spring and summer. *Fabaceae (Leguminosae)* **4**

Pelargonium cordifolium [P. cordatum] (Heart-leaf Geranium) Many people are confused by the names. The common name for Pelargonium is Geranium, which is a different but related genus. This shrub grows five feet tall, with clusters of purple flowers in spring and summer. *Geraniaceae* **6**

Pelargonium hybrid (Scented Geranium) One of many of this group of Geraniums which are grown primarily for the attractive, fragrant foliage. Each variety has a different scent - apple, nutmeg, lemon, etc. *Geraniaceae* **30**

Pelargonium tomentosum (Peppermint Geranium) The velvety leaves have a strong peppermint aroma when rubbed. The 'Chocolate Mint' cultivar, a hybrid between *P. tomentosum* and *P. quercifolium*, has an attractive brown pattern on the leaves, but lacks the scent. *Geraniaceae* **25**

Pennisetum 'Eaton Canyon' (Dwarf Red Fountain Grass) This is a smaller version of the common Purple Pennisetum, growing 2 to 3 feet tall. It is more inclined to be evergreen, but is not as colorful. It has similar red-bronze flower plumes in summer. *Poaceae* **22**

Penstemon hybrid (Garden Penstemon) Many colorful hybrids have been developed from a number of species native to the southwestern US. They are all drought tolerant and range in height from 18 inches to 4 feet with flowers of red, purple, pink, white and blue. *Scrophulariaceae* **22**

Perovskia atriplicifolia (Russian Sage) Native to western and central Asia, this drought tolerant member of the mint family is valuable in the perennial border for its electric blue flowers and ferny gray foliage. It dies down completely in winter. *Lamiaceae (Labiatae)* **22**

Phalaris arundinacea 'Picta' (Ribbon Grass) A grass of garden origin with green and cream-colored stripes It grows 18 to 24 inches tall and spreads by runners, though not aggressively. White flowers appear in late spring and early summer. 'Feesy's Form' has pink stripes which turn to cream color. *Poaceae* **18**

Philadelphus mexicanus (Mexican Mock Orange) An evergreen member of this popular genus of fragrant shrubs. Unlike its temperate climate cousins, it is a vining shrub which spreads by stolons; it can reach 10 feet in height, spreading indefinitely. *Hydrangeaceae* **13, 32**

Phlomis fruticosa (Jerusalem Sage) From the eastern Mediterranean, this shrubby perennial has soft gray-green leaves and vertical stems with whorls of yellow flowers in abundance in spring and summer, with a scattering of blooms the rest of the year. *Lamiaceae (Labiatae)* **19**

Phoenix canariensis (Canary Island Date Palm) Thick-trunked feather palm reaching 75 feet in height. The dense crown spanning up to 25 feet, consisting of arching fronds with sharp spines at the base of each frond. White flowers develop into colorful large clusters of orange fruit, any time of year. *Arecaceae (Palmae)* **All over**

Phoenix reclinata (Senegal Date Palm) Multi-stem palm from western Africa with trunks to 30 feet tall. A graceful landscape specimen in near frost-free climates. *Arecaceae (Palmae)* **19**

Phormium tenax (New Zealand Flax) This strident accent plant grows naturally in conditions ranging from marshes to dry ground. It is a tough perennial with sword-shaped leaves, hybridized in many colors and sizes from 18 inches to 8 feet tall. *Agavaceae* **10, 11**

Pistacia chinensis (Chinese Pistache) Deciduous tree to 40 feet tall with an equal spread, though usually much smaller here. The foliage turns orange and red in fall about the same time the pink fruit appears. In China, young shoots and leaves are eaten. *Anacardiaceae* **13**

Pittosporum tobira (Tobira, Mock Orange) A broadleaf evergreen shrub from Japan which can be trained as a small multi-stem tree. It has thick, shiny leaves and very fragrant, yellow/white flowers in spring. *Pittosporacee* **24**

Pittosporum undulatum (Victorian Box) From New South Wales and Queensland, Australia. Rapid-growing tree usually used as a boundary screen hedge. Clusters of white flowers provide wonderful night fragrance in February. *Pittosporaceae* **1**

Plecostachys serpyllifolia (Licorice Plant) A South African native with small, wooly, pale gray leaves. It is a woody perennial which can reach 4 feet in height and 8 feet in diameter in one season. *Asteraceae (Compositae)* **17**

Pleioblastus From Asia, a running bamboo, but not agressive. It has vertical, green leaves and grows to 4 feet. *Poaceae* **35**

Pleioblastus variegata (Dwarf Whitestripe Bamboo) A running Bamboo from Asia growing only 2 to 3 feet tall. It makes a lovely tall groundcover in part shade - if contained. *Poaceae* **27, 35**

Plumbago auriculata [P. capensis] (Plumbago) A tenacious plant from South Africa which will easily take over by spreading underground, re-seeding and climbing anything within reach. It has light green leaves and pale blue or white flowers. A recent cultivar has a more intense true-blue flower. *Plumbaginaceae* **32, 33**

Polygonum capitatum (Pinkhead Knotweed) A groundcover for frost-free areas. It is usually less than 1 inch deep with purple veined leaves and little, round, pink flowers through-out the year. *Polygonaceae* **39**

Pontederia cordata (Azure Pickerel Weed) An aquatic plant from eastern North America with large, thick arrowhead shaped leaves and stalks of blue flowers. *Pontederiaceae* **25, 26, 27**

Prunus campanulata (Taiwan Flowering Cherry) A subtropical cherry with a banded trunk and brilliant rose-pink blossoms in pendant clusters in January. *Rosaceae* **8, 11**

Prunus dulcis [P. amygdalus] (Sweet Almond) From Asia Minor and North Africa. The tree grows to 20 to 30 feet tall and as wide, with sharp branch tips. Pale lavender flowers burst forth in February and almost cover the branches. Grown commercially for the nuts which are the seed of a peach-like fruit. *Rosaceae* **33**

Prunus persica (Peach, Flowering Peach) A small deciduous tree, probably from Asia. It grows 15 to 25 feet tall with an equal spread and has a spectacular display of flowers which cover the branches in January or February. There are many named varieties in white, pink, red and 'Peppermint'. *Rosaceae* **33**

Psoralea pinnata (Blue Pea, Scurf Pea) An open, upright shrub 10-12 feet tall from South Africa. It has dark green needle-like leaves and clusters of half-inch blue and white grape scented flowers. *Fabaceae (Leguminosae)* **7**

Pteridium aquilinum (Bracken, Brake Fern) Native to much of the world, this fern has vertical stems, from spreading roots, which rise 3 to 5 feet and are topped by coarse, horizontal fronds. *Polypodiaceae* **10**

Pyracantha 'Tiny Tim' (Dwarf Firethorn, Pyracantha) A diminutive cultivar from a clan of giant shrubs from Asia and the Mediterranean. It is less than 3 feet tall and has red berries and very few thorns. *Rosaceae* **17**

Pyrus kawakamii (Evergreen Pear) Almost evergreen is more accurate, with dark green, wavy-edge leaves, which turn red as they fall. A bare tree in December indicates a spectacular display of cloud-like white blossoms in January and February. *Rosaceae* **Garden Street**

Quercus agrifolia (Coast Live Oak) Co-official Santa Barbara City tree with Jacaranda, this evergreen member of the Oak-Beech family is one of several tree-size native California Oaks. Some specimens in the wild are 50 feet tall with a spread of over 100 feet. *Fagaceae* **1**

Roldana petasitis [Senecio petasitis] (Velvet Groundsel) From Mexico, this large shrubby perennial has velvety, notched, dark green leaves. In early winter deep burgundy flower buds develop and open to clusters of bright yellow daisies. *Asteraceae (Compositae)* **4, 5**

Romneya coulteri (Matilija Poppy) A native Southern California perennial which can grow 6 feet tall in one season. The stems are clothed with blue-gray divided leaves topped with 6 inch "fried egg" blossoms from spring into summer. *Papaveraceae* **5**

Rosa bracteata 'Mermaid' (Mermaid Rose) A very thorny vine from China with glossy disease-free foliage and large single yellow flowers year-round. It can reach 50 feet in the right situation. As the common name indicates, this rose is quite happy growing next to the ocean. *Rosaceae* **11**

Rosa 'Cecile Brunner' (Sweetheart Rose) An old favorite, it was a popular boutonnière flower in the late 1800s because the tiny buds are perfectly formed and have a nice fragrance. The climbing

form is used as a landscape plant; it's main blooming season is March, with a scattering of blossoms through summer, and another burst in fall. *Rosaceae* **22**

Rosa 'Mme. Alfred Carrier' A vigorous climbing rose which dates back to 1879. Small blush-white, sweet scented flowers are abundant in the spring with a scattering until fall. It can reach 30 feet in height and sometimes climbs high in trees. *Rosaceae* **22**

Rosmarinus officinalis 'Lockwood de Forest' (Prostrate Rosemary) Honoring this Santa Barbara landscape architect, this rosemary has lighter green foliage and paler blue flowers than the common prostrate rosemary. *Lamiaceae (Labiatae)* **15, 17**

Ruscus hypoglossum (Butcher's Broom) A rugged, undemanding groundcover for shaded areas. This spreading plant has unusual flattened branches instead of leaves. Inconspicuous white flowers in the center of the "leaf" develop into marble size red berries *Liliaceae* **1**

Salix matsudana 'Tortuosa' (Corkscrew Willow, Dragon Claw Willow) Fast-growing tree 30 feet tall by 20 feet wide with twisted, spiraling branch patterns. It weeps gracefully and is attractive in all seasons. The bare branches are used by florists. *Salicaceae* **3**

Salvia guaranitica 'Costa Rica Blue' (Anise-scented Sage) Big, tropical-looking woody perennial with large leaves and flowers of violet-blue on a plant 5 to 7 feet tall and wide. *Lamiaceae (Labiatae)* **23**

Salvia sagittata (Arrow-leaf Sage) An evergreen perennial from high in the Andes. It grows 3 to 5 feet tall with green arrow-shaped leaves and spikes of blue flowers in summer. *Lamiaceae (Labiatae)* **7**

Salvia uliginosa (Bog Sage) A native of moist areas in South America. This sage grows 4 to 5 feet tall with light green foliage and sky-blue flowers, spring to fall. It spreads by rhizomes and needs a root barrier in moist soils. *Lamiaceae (Labiatae)* **23**

Scabiosa columbaria (Pincushion Flower) *Scabiosa* earned its botanical name during the Middle Ages in Europe, where it was used to treat festering sores, or scabies. It is an evergreen mat-forming perennial, available in pink or lavender-blue named varieties. *Dipsacaceae* **22**

Scilla peruviana (Cuban Lily) Both names are misleading because it comes from Southern Europe and North Africa. Floppy green leaves in winter are topped by large, flattened, pure blue flower clusters in spring. *Liliaceae* **7**

Sedum dendroideum (Stonecrop) A succulent from Mexico which grows 2 feet tall and spreads indefinitely as the stems take root when they touch the ground. It has light green, rounded leaves and yellow flowers in spring. *Crassulaceae* **18**

Senecio mandraliscae [Kleinia mandraliscae] (Kleinia) A clumping succulent plant, from South Africa, with round, blue-green, upright leaves. The white flowers in summer are not significant. *Asteraceae (Compositae)* **4**

Senecio serpens [Kleinia repens] (Blue Chalk Sticks, Kleinia) Lower growing than *S. mandraliscae*, with thicker leaves. *Asteraceae (Compositae)* **15**

Senna didymobotrya [Cassia nairobensis] (Cassia) An evergreen shrub from East Africa with an unpleasant odor when the leaves are bruised. It grows 6 to 8 feet tall and wider with compound dark green leaves and large, upright clusters of yellow flowers during winter and spring. *Fabaceae (Leguminosae)* **35**

Senna splendida [Cassia splendida] (Golden Wonder) Senna An open-growing, evergreen shrub from Brazil to 10 feet tall with gold flowers in fall. Fabaceae *(Leguminosae)* **42**

Setaria palmifolia (Palm Grass) From India, a clumping grass 4 to 6 feet tall with pleated leaves, resembling palm tree seedlings. The white flower spikes rise above the foliage in summer, resulting in seedlings—everywhere. *Poaceae* **35**

Sparaxis tricolor (Harlequin Flower) Another member of the Iris family from South Africa. It is at home in a summer dry setting, and will naturalize there. Short, grassy foliage emerges in winter with multi-colored flowers in February. *Iridaceae* **23**

Spiraea cantoniensis 'Flore Pleno', 'Lanceolata,' [S. reevesii] (Bridal Wreath) A large shrub from China. It is semi-evergreen in mild winter climates where it becomes a spectacular fountain of white from early March into April. *Rosaceae* **25**

Stachys byzantina (Lamb's Ears) From the Caucasus and Iran, this low perennial has wooly gray, almost white, foliage and spikes of lavender flowers in spring. *Lamiaceae (Labiatae)* **4**

Syagrus romanzoffiana [Arecastrum romanzoffianum, Cocos plumosa] (Queen Palm) A straight, gray trunk palm From Brazil growing to 60 feet. The leaflets grow all round the midrib, for a fluffy effect. Creamy-white flower clusters are followed by heavy clusters of orange fruit. *Arecaceae (Palmae)* **17**

Syzygium australe [S. paniculatum, Eugenia myrtifolia] (Eugenia, Australian Brush Cherry) Queensland and New South Wales. It can grow to 90 feet with a trunk 6 feet in diameter. Usually seen as a sheared hedge; it is easily recognized by its shiny dark green leaves with red new growth. The magenta fruit is edible. *Myrtaceae* **Arrellaga Street**

Tabebuia chrysotricha (Golden Trumpet Tree) From Central America, where it grows tall and literally bursts into blossom overnight with the first rain of the season. In Southern California it has a brief but spectacular show of electric yellow flowers late winter to early spring. This small deciduous tree is rather inconspicuous the rest of the year. *Bignoniaceae* **13**

Tabebuia impetiginosa (Pink Trumpet Tree) Although it can reach 50 feet in its native South American environment, here it is a small deciduous tree up to 25 feet tall. Like the golden trumpet tree, it has a brief but spectacular display of blossoms on bare branches in early spring. *Bignoniaceae* **11**

Tagetes lemmonii (Bush Marigold, Copper Canyon Daisy) A cheerful winter bloomer from north-central Mexico. The leaves on this 4 foot by 5 foot shrub have a pleasant scent when brushed. The "Kodak" yellow flowers are typical of single marigolds. *Asteraceae (Compositae)* **9**

Tecoma stans [Stenolobium stans] (Yellow Elder, Yellow Trumpet Flower) Large shrub or small tree from Florida to Guatemala. It has light evergreen foliage and yellow, tubular flowers from spring through fall. It is one parent of *T. × smithii.* *Bignoniaceae* **6**

Tecoma × smithii (Orange Bells) Large multi-trunk shrub 8 to 12 feet tall and wide. It has light green compound leaves and soft orange, tubular flowers in summer and fall which attract hummingbirds. *Bignoniaceae* **30**

Tecomaria capensis 'Aurea' [Tecoma capensis 'Aurea'] (Cape Honeysuckle) A vining shrub from South Africa. The species has red-orange flowers and is a vigorous vine that can grow to 30 feet in trees. This yellow-flowered cultivar has lighter green foliage and is more compact. Orange and buff colored varieties are available. *Bignoniaceae* **30**

Thunbergia gregorii [T. gibsonii] (Orange Clock Vine) A vigorous, frost-tender vine whose fuzzy arrowhead shaped leaves are covered by intense orange flowers year-round. It will readily cover a chain-link fence or sprawl on the ground. *Acanthaceae* **18**

Thymus vulgaris (Common Thyme) An herb from the Mediterranean which serves a double purpose as a groundcover and seasoning for food. The species has gray-green leaves and pale lavender flowers in spring and summer. Several cultivars have been developed with different foliage colors and flavors. *Lamiaceae (Labiatae)* **23**

Tibouchina urvilleana (Princess Flower) Purple velvet best describes the 3 inch single flowers of this semi-tropical Brazilian. It grows as an open shrub 6 to 8 feet tall and almost as wide. The ribbed leaves are also velvety and develop red tinges when grown in full sun. *Melastomaceae* **26**

Tipuana tipu (Tipu Tree) A widely spreading tree from South America which grows rapidly, 30 to 40 feet tall and 60 feet wide. The compound leaves fall in late March and new foliage arrives in May, followed by golden flowers which continue through July. It is a wonderful shade tree, especially when the delicate flowers fall in the lightest breeze. *Fabaceae (Leguminosae)* **13, 25, 27**

Toona sinensis 'Flamingo' [Cedrela sinensis] (Cigar Box Tree) From China, where it can grow to 50 feet tall. In Santa Barbara it is 15 to 20 feet and suckers to become an attractive clump. From its bare, linear winter aspect, pink foliage emerges in spring, changing to creamy yellow then a medium green for summer. The wood is used to make cigar boxes. *Meliaceae* **10**

Trachycarpus fortunei (Windmill Palm) A small fan palm from China with a slender, hairy trunk. It is an unusual site in winter, in Central Europe, with snow covered fronds. *Arecaceae (Palmae)* **3**

Tropaeolum majus (Nasturtium) A familiar annual vine from Peru. It has large waterlily-like leaves and yellow, orange or red flowers in winter and spring—summer if watered. The watercress flavored leaves and flowers are used in salads. *Tropaeolaceae* **39**

Typha spp. (Cat Tail) Wind-borne seeds start new plants in every body of water, or damp ground. A plant with a strong verticality in the leaves and fuzzy brown cattails. *Typhaceae* **26**

Viola odorata (Sweet Violet) The legendary violet beloved for its delicate purple flowers and distinctive fragrance. A lovely woodland plant which has been developed into many named cultivars. *Violaceae* **37**

Washingtonia robusta (Mexican Fan Palm) From Baja California and very drought tolerant. The ball of fronds on a slender 80 to 100 foot trunk have made it a signature skyline tree of Southern California. *Arecaceae (Palmae)* **3**

Wedelia trilobata (Yellow buttons) Tropical America. A frost-tender groundcover growing 18 to 24 inches tall, or more if it has something to climb. Little yellow daisies are sprinkled on the dark green, toothed foliage year-round. This is the most prevalent groundcovers of the tropical world. *Asteraceae (Compositae)* **33**

Wisteria sinensis (Chinese Wisteria) A vigorous vine which climbs by twining. In the garden it is trained along the top of a stone wall and on the pergola which has been a backdrop for many weddings. Lavender flower clusters with a wonderful fragrance unfurl in March. *Fabaceae (Leguminosae)* **21, 29, 31**

Woodwardia radicans (European Chain Fern) A species from Southern Europe which is similar to our native chain fern, but more refined. The medium green fronds grow 3 to 4 feet long and arch gracefully. When the tip reaches the ground, a bud on the underside takes root and starts a new plant. *Blechnaceae* **25**

Xylosma congesta 'Compacta' (Dwarf Xylosma) From China, a smaller version, 8 feet by 8 feet, of a large shrub/small tree. The yellow-green leaves with red edges on a full-foliaged shrub have made this a basic landscape plant. It has wicked thorns. *Flacourtiaceae* **23, 24**

Zephyranthes candida (Fairy Lily, Zephyr Flower, Rain Lily) A grassy plant from Central and South America which grows from bulbs. In fall, with the slightest bit of rain, white flowers appear, literally overnight, to cover the foliage. Sprinklers do not provide the full effect. *Amaryllidaceae* **6**

index of plants

acknowledgments

With deep gratitude I acknowledge the invaluable support and encouragement of my family and friends. Special credit is due to my daughter, Katie Hatch, my staunchest advocate, and an invaluable resource, who provided creative insight and sensitive advice. Thanks also to my son, Paul, whose faith in the project was a precious gift. I appreciate the advice and graphical expertise of son-in-law, Jim Hatch. His approval buoyed my confidence. Barbara Harlow, you were my inspiration. My mentors, Tana Sommer and Barry Spacks, both deserve special recognition for the kindness and grace they share with so many. Irwin Lunianski, my good friend, you believed in me and encouraged me to dream; your unwavering support sustained the effort.

Thanks also to: the talented group at Media 27: Mike Verbois, Shukri Farhad, and Judi Muller; Joan Tapper, the "light touch" editing wizard; the City of Santa Barbara Parks and Recreation Department, Billie Goodnick and Kathleen Sullivan; the Santa Barbara Botanic Garden, particularly J. Robert Haller, Ph.D., Jeff Cope, Dieter Wilken, Ph.D., and Nancy Johnson. Along the way many wonderful people have advised and assisted: Arthur Gaudi, Carol Valentine, Joanna Bard Newton, Kellam de Forest, John Alexander, Jim Owen, Clay Tedeschi, Eleanor Beronius, Shelly Ruston and Anne Lowenkopf—to each of you, my deepest gratitude for your help.

Kudos to Ralph Clevenger whose brilliant photographs tell the story of Alice's Garden more effectively than words ever could.

I also want to thank my husband, Grant Castleberg, for his unstinting assistance and particularly for the impressive plant list. On behalf of all the people whose lives have been enriched by his landscape designs, I dedicate this book to Grant, with all my love.

Anne-Marie Castleberg

Every effort has been made to obtain permission from the appropriate parties. If any mistakes have been made we will be happy to correct them. We gratefully acknowledge permission to print the copyrighted material listed below.

SOURCES AND PERMISSIONS

"Agriculture in the City—El Mirasol Educational Farm," Community Environmental Council, Inc, Santa Barbara, 1975.

Beresdford, Hattie M., "El Mirasol—Graceful Swan to Ominous Albatross," *Noticias—Quarterly Magazine of the Santa Barbara Historical Society, XLVII. No 1* (Spring 2001), p30.

Berry, Wendell, From "I," *A Timbered Choir: The Sabbath Poems 1979-1997.* Counterpoint, Washington, D.C., copyright 1998. Reprinted by permission of Counterpoint Press, a member of Perseus Books, L.L.C.

Campbell, Joseph, *The Power of Myth with Bill Moyers,* Betty Sue Flowers, Editor, Doubleday, 1988, p92.

Carson, Rachel, from *The Sense of Wonder,* copyright 1956 by Rachel L. Carson, copyright renewed 1984 Roger Christie, reprinted by permission of Frances Collin, Trustee.

Dunn, Richard, "A Dubious Heritage," book review, *The East Hampton Star,* November 1926.

Gookin, John (editor), *Nols Wildresness Wisdom: Quotes for Inspirational Exploration,* Stackpole Books, Pennsylvania, 2003. Selected quotes reprinted with permission from NOLS.

Ignatow, David, From: "In the Garden," (p69), "One Leaf," (p81), "Three in Transition," (p90), Whisper to the Earth; From "Autumn Leaves" (p81), *Against the Evidence: Selected Poems 1934 - 1994,* copyright 1994 by David Ignatow and reprinted by permission of Wesleyan University Press.

John Ruskin, "Modern Painters," vol. III, part IV, ch 17, *Collected Works,* George Allen, London, 1903, pp386 - 387.

Pico Iyer, Quote printed with permission of the author.

Sarton, May, "Old Trees," (p38), from *Collected Poems 1930 - 1993,* copyright 1993, 1988, 1984, 1974 by May Sarton. Used by permission of W. W. Norton & Company, Inc. p97, from *Journal of Solitude,* W. W. Norton & Company, New York, 1973, p34.

Shoson, (Kenneth Yasuda), From "Irises," *A Pepper Pod—A Haiku Sampler,* Charles E. Tuttle Co, Rutland, Vermont. Used by permission of Tuttle Publishing, Rutland, Vermont.

Sommer, Tana, from "Noontime Bench," unpublished chapbook. Used with permission of the poet.

Spacks, Barry, From "Poem Left In a Bottle on a Hilltop" (p13), *Brief Sparrow,* Illuminati, Los Angeles, 1988. From "Black Star Yearning," (p44), *Regarding Woman—Poems by Barry Spacks,* Cherry Grove Collections, copyright Barry Spacks 2004. Used with permission of the poet.

Stétié, Salah, *Lumiere sur lumiere,* Les Cahiers de L'Egare, Le Revest-les-Eaux, 1992. Used with permission of Bloodaxe Books, England.

Wagoner, David, "Lost" from *Traveling Light: Collected and New Poems,* copyright 1999 by David Wagoner. Used with permission of the poet and the University of Illinois Press.

Wilcox, Ella Wheeler, "The World's Need," *The Little Book of American Poets: 1787-1900,* Ed. Jessie B. Rittenhouse. Cambridge: Riverside Press, 1915.

William Carlos Williams, "Silence," from *Collected Later Poems 1939 - 1962,* Volume II, copyright 1953 by William Carlos Williams. Reprinted by permission of New Directions Publishing Corp.

PHOTOGRAPHY CREDITS

All Photographs By Ralph Clevenger Except the following:

P10   Aerial view of park site, image provided by William Dewey.

P11   Elizabeth de Forest, image provided by Kellam de Forest.

P11   Reginald Faletti, image provided by the Santa Barbara Museum of Art.

P11   Francis Price, image provided by Price Postel & Parma LLP.

P14   Haley and Wackenreuder Map, image provided by the City of Santa Barbara Parks and Recreation Department. Graphic enhancement by Jim Hatch, Hatch Illustrations.

P15   Mary Miles Herter, El Mirasol Hotel, the collection of the Santa Barbara Historic Society. Graphic enhancement by Jim Hatch, Hatch Illustrations.

P16   El Mirasol Hotel photos, the collection of the Santa Barbara Historic Society. Images provided by City of Santa Barbara Parks and Recreation Department. Graphic enhancement by Jim Hatch, Hatch Illustrations.

P17   El Mirasol Condominiums, image provided by the City of Santa Barbara Parks and Recreation Department.

P18   CEC Farm, from 1975 report, "Agriculture in the City," Community Environmental Council.

P23   Construction photo. Reprinted with permission from the Santa Barbara News-Press. Photo credit: Steve Malone/Santa Barbara News-Press.

P43   Couple on bench, Clint Weisman Studio.

P43   Couple under Jacaranda, photo by Katie Hatch.

P120   David Park, image provided by Eleanor Beronius.

P121   Alice Keck Park, image provided by Santa Barbara Cottage Hospital.

Var: Pre-construction and construction photos by Grant Castleberg.

Var: 30 (child), 42, 43(children), 52, 88 (turtle) by Anne-Marie Castleberg.

*or 20 years now, Alice Keck Park
has been my special solace, my
secret refuge at the center of Santa
Barbara. It's where I go to think
out whatever I'm writing, it's
where I've marked small memorial
services for friends I've loved and
lost, it's where I stroll as I write
this to watch the children pointing
at the pond, the people performing
tai chi under a tree, the families
enjoying a circle of sunlight. There
are many reasons for being grateful
for living in Santa Barbara, but
Alice Keck—small, exquisite,
thoughtful and miraculously
varied—is one of the deepest ones,
for me. It is a perfect emblem of
our city at its best.*

PICO IYER